The

Gentlemen's
Society *of*
Angling

Alli,

First peace along

gentle flowing waters.

Jay Hill

The

Gentlemen's
Society *of*
Angling

JAY HILL

PRUETT

Pruett Publishing Company
Boulder, Colorado

Pruett Publishing Company
7464 Arapahoe Road, Suite A9
Boulder, Colorado 80303
www.pruettpublishing.com

Printed in the United States of America
11 10 09 08 07 06 05 04 03 02   5 4 3 2

Library of Congress Cataloging-in-Publication Data

Hill, Jay, 1952–
    The gentlemen's society of angling / Jay Hill.
        p. cm.
    ISBN 0-87108-920-3
    I. Title.

PS3608.I43 G4 2001
813'.6—dc21   2001031924

Cover and book design by Studio Signorella
Book composition by Lyn Chaffee

To Lisa,
who lovingly tolerates my passion for fly fishing
and Lauren and Jamie,
who add to the beauty of cold mountain streams

The Discovery

The remark Kelly had once made when we were eating lunch by the Platte River fairly summed up our passion: "You know, there's never a time when I'm not fishing—just days when I can't do it in water."

I had no particular reason to resist Kelly's suggestion that I clear the calendar for a few days, hop in the car, and come spend some time in the limestone creeks of Ligonier in Pennsylvania. Just because I was a westerner didn't mean I preferred the more raucous and powerful rivers of northern Colorado. Waters like the North Platte are simply what's available where I live. But the streams back in Pennsylvania, according to Kelly, were the stuff of legends. Gentle flows. Clean. Stream-born brook trout. If fly fishing has roots, these streams are among those where they were laid down. Soon enough, fifteen hundred miles of road beckoned and I headed for Kelly's place.

As I steered the Toyota east out of Latrobe, Pennsylvania, the small, rolling Laurel Mountains of the area began closing in around me. The highway between Latrobe and Ligonier winds through country steeped in history. From the early days of settlements, this section of western Pennsylvania was the edge of the frontier. Fort Ligonier has been fully restored and sits prominently in the middle of this small burg to remind everyone of the great battles that English, French, and native forces waged for control of the area. In the mid-1700s, Fort Ligonier successfully fended off an attack by the French and Indians from the nearby Loyalhanna village, despite the arrival two days late of a Virginia regiment led by British Lieutenant George Washington. It was also from Fort Ligonier that a successful campaign was mounted against Fort Duquesne, located at the confluence of the Monongahela, Allegheny, and Ohio rivers in what is now Pittsburgh. Eventually Fort Ligonier became a way station along the turnpike from Philadelphia to Fort Pitt.

The highway dramatically split, each fork hugging a carved shelf on a series of opposite hillsides cut by a small river at their base. As soon as the woods thinned and I saw the water, my right foot reacted in customary fashion—it lifted off the gas pedal. A friend pointed out this peculiarity during a trip to Wyoming where we were crossing streams and rivers one after another. Mike, my partner that day, claimed he was suffering whiplash from the bucking of the car. I know why it happens. I cannot resist looking at water. Whether it's twenty feet, twenty yards, or two hundred yards away, I must look. I begin immediately searching for holds for fish. Hell, there are times I'm trying to see if I can spot the fish themselves. It's a ridiculous habit and one I cannot in any rational way explain. But neither do I feel guilty or embarrassed by it. The next time Mike and I took a trip together, I brought him a wraparound neck brace, tossed it over to him when he got in the car, and said, "Here, you may need this."

Now I was focusing on the stream a hundred feet or so below me winding its way down the course it had cut through this series of hills. I liked very much what I was seeing. Small pools. Holding water behind polished rocks. Periodic weed beds. The temptation to pull off the road and grab my rod was genuine, but I lacked a fishing license. Also, I had four days ahead of me and hadn't even seen Kelly yet. Eyes straight ahead. Foot on the gas. Patience. Patience. Eventually the two sections of the roadway again merged, and the stream moved off to my right under a bridge and out of view. There is truth in the phrase "out of sight, out of mind." As soon as the water was no longer visible, I began thinking about whether I could find Kelly's house.

Kelly had told me that another twenty-five miles or so ahead I would see a sign pointing left that said Highway 58. He said I couldn't miss it. I didn't. Everything went smoothly until about a half mile down Highway 58. Now, am I supposed to take the right or the left fork of the road? What did he say? I remember he said a left on 58, then another left, and then a right. Or was that a left, right, left? Damn, where are those directions? I began rummaging through a bag on the seat, all the while, of course, continuing along the winding roads that were taking me farther and farther into the hills. Once I did locate his directions, I was so lost that none of the markers he'd mentioned appeared ahead. Damn.

At times like this, I have to admit to myself that I do stupid things. I pulled the car into a gravel drive, turned around, and headed back the way I came. If I could find my way back to the highway, I could start over. I had paid enough attention to recognize the highway sign pointing in opposite directions to Latrobe and Ligonier as I neared it. I pulled into the parking lot of the Treetop Tavern to study my notes, then turned around and again headed back in the direction from which I had just come. Somehow, some way, over the course of the next fifteen minutes, I again circled my way back to the Treetop's parking lot. I thought, okay, admit you're lost and find a phone.

I pulled up to the Treetop figuring there'd be a phone inside. As I approached the door, I spotted a row of at least twenty Harleys parked in front of the tavern. Oh, great, a biker bar! I ventured inside. The place was pretty decent. The typical neon beer signs hung from the wall. Round metal-rimmed plastic-top tables were positioned around a well-used pool table. But the layout didn't matter right now, because I had drawn the attention of every face attached to the row of bodies perched on the bar stools. Almost in unison, every head turned to see who had entered the Treetop. I'm sure the smile I plastered on my face revealed my discomfort, but at times like this the best thing to do is push ahead. My attire certainly was out of place. Khaki shorts, a T-shirt, and sandals were no match for basic black. I felt like the L. L. Bean–Harley Davidson poster boy.

I spotted a phone at the end of the bar. As I dropped in a quarter and dialed Kelly's number, I watched the game the Treetop patrons were playing at the bar. Each player was drawing a beer-bottle cap from a bucket the bartender held. The player would look at the inside of the cap, then either shove it into the tray running along the back edge of the bar, or slide some money farther out on the bar and set the cap on top of it. Ahh, your basic Saturday morning beer fest and poker party. Geez, and I was worried. I heard the phone picked up on the other end.

"Kelly? Yeah, hi. No, I'm down here in the bar at the corner where I turn to find your place."

I was glad no one at the bar could hear Kelly's emphatic response. "You're inside the Treetop?"

The tone in his voice made my alarm button ring. "Uh-huh," I said casually so as not to reveal my anxiety. "Can you come meet me down here? I can't figure out how to find your house. Great." I hung up the phone.

By this time, the money along the bar had been set down in front of a guy at the far end, and the bottle caps were being tossed back into the bucket. As I walked to the door, I waved tentatively toward the bartender and said, "Thanks." There was no acknowledgment of my gesture. In fact, my presence was of less importance to the poker players than the sign hanging above the door that said, "If you can read this, you ain't done." Well, yes I could, and yes I was.

As I pulled my car to the far side of the parking lot to wait for Kelly, I had a vision of me as Pee Wee Herman in *Pee Wee's Big Adventure* bumping the end bike and watching the whole row domino down on top of each other. I settled back in my seat, but found myself occasionally peering into the rearview mirror half expecting the guys inside to come after me. Of course, they couldn't care less about me. Thank you very much. I also wondered if they sat at the bar in the same order as they parked their bikes. Ten minutes later, Kelly's Jeep pulled alongside me.

"So, how are your buddies in the Treetop?" he asked grinning.

"They all said they missed you and asked if I knew what you wanted for your birthday," I shot back. He laughed. I tailed Kelly as he headed into the hills and realized once we pulled into his driveway that I would have never found this place. I hadn't even been close.

I had seen pictures of Kelly and Lisa's house, but pictures didn't do it justice. No photograph could grasp the views of the valley from the front windows. No wonder the place was called Hawk Ridge. Their home sat atop one of the highest points in the area, giving me a feeling of what a raptor might see perched on a branch.

"Great view," was my lackluster compliment.

"Yeah, we like it." Lisa slid her arm inside Kelly's to pull him closer.

"So, old buddy, you finally ready to do some real trout fishing?" Kelly asked, stating the obvious.

"That's what I'm here for."

"Good. Let's go!"

"Right now?" I asked, taken off guard.

"Why not?" Kelly said matter-of-factly.

What could I say? This was classic Kelly and one reason I had grown so fond of him. Every moment was something to grab and go with. Sometimes his energy was overwhelming, but it also was invigorating. It took me only a few minutes to sort through my gear and transfer it to his Jeep, and within twenty minutes of my arrival, I was heading out again.

"So, tell me about the creek I drove along on the way over here from Latrobe," I said as we pulled out of the driveway.

"That's the Loyalhanna. It's pretty good fishing at times, but it's also suffered quite a bit from running through the towns. The local Trout Unlimited club is working on it, but there are still too many other folks who don't seem to care about the pollution they contribute," Kelly explained.

"Hey, old buddy, where are we headed?" I finally thought to ask.

"Stonycreek. It's up in the mountains a little way and hasn't been impacted much. All of the fish are native, and there are several spots where we can walk in and you can see what Pennsylvania limestone creek fishing is all about."

The river was only about thirty miles east of Ligonier, but it still was a forty-five-minute drive because there are no direct routes. We had to go north before we could go south. Also, we had to stop to get my fishing license. Soon we reached a highway pull-off and stopped. We slipped on our waders, grabbed the rods and vests, and headed down a path that paralleled the road before turning into the woods. During the walk to the water, Kelly explained that it was common on rivers like this one to get an early sulphur mayfly hatch. If one happened during the late afternoon, we'd be in for some great dry-fly action.

As soon as we stepped into the water, I realized why Kelly had insisted that I visit him. The spring bloom was at its height, and the deep purples and reds of the wild rhododendrons were everywhere. From midstream, the woods looked as if someone had splattered a brush full of paint into the undergrowth. It was far different from what I was used to back in Colorado, where only sporadic tufts of Indian paintbrush added color to the sagebrush-dominated landscape. Also, the deciduous forest here contrasted sharply with the pine groves back home.

Over the course of the afternoon, Kelly taught me the tricks of fishing this type of stream, and by dusk we had both released several beautiful brookies and small rainbows. On the drive home, he told me he wouldn't be available to fish tomorrow until the afternoon, but if I wanted to go out on my own, he would draw me a map to a spot where he could join me at noon. That evening we finalized those plans, and at breakfast the next morning Lisa went over the directions with me once more.

I located the spot where Kelly was sending me without a problem, although I did check my plan with a clerk at a convenience store when I stopped for another cup of coffee. As I rigged up for the day, I figured I'd leave my lunch in the car, since I had promised Kelly I'd meet him there rather than on the water. The stream where he had sent me was much like the Stonycreek, fairly small in width and heavily tree-lined. Though Kelly had promised me that Laurel Creek was probably the best stream around and a place where even rookies could catch fish, somebody forgot to tell this to the fish. For more than two hours, I tried different strategies. I fished dry flies, attractors, nymphs, emergers—at one point I even put on a dropper, which for a stream of this size is like using a down-rigger. Despite all these efforts, only two fish saw fit to cooperate.

I glanced at my watch and realized I was in for a long morning. It was 10:00 A.M., the fish weren't hungry, and Kelly was at least two hours away from lending assistance. What to do? I climbed up on the bank and took a seat on a small rock to think. At least I'd brought along a candy bar. I sat there, Mounds bar in hand, trying to figure out what to do when I looked across the stream and realized I had a great opportunity to photograph the flowers.

After hiding my rod, I began wandering along the banks of the river taking pictures of the blooms that seemed more radiant with each step farther into the trees. White mountain laurel blossoms were spreading their fragrance through the woods as if they wanted to scent every bush and tree. It was working—the more deeply I breathed, the more consumed I was with the aroma. I felt like Flower, the blossom-sniffing skunk in Disney's movie *Bambi*. The stream that had frustrated me all morning was aptly named. As I wandered farther into the woods, snapping a shot here and there, I spotted what appeared to be a roof and a wall of timber up on a small incline, barely visible behind a growth of brush. Circling the structure to the left, I began to identify it as a cabin now being consumed by the woods and the insects. The walls were constructed of logs with some of the pitch remaining in the gaps between them. The west wall at one time must have had a smaller room attached to it, for there was an opening in the main wall that was far larger than a doorway. As I approached for a closer look, I saw an outline of a stone foundation and some planks of siding on the ground. On the north side of the cabin I found a pile of fieldstones that at one time must have formed the above-roof section of the chimney. The part of it that had not fallen was still attached to the structure. The east wall contained two openings for windows. Here I could get close enough to peer inside. As my eyes adjusted to the darkness, I could begin to make out the details of the interior.

The main door of the cabin was located in the corner immediately to my left. I walked around to it, but access was impossible because the bushes and ivy had grown impenetrably thick. There were only two ways I could get inside—one through the opening where the small room had collapsed, the other through the window casement. I chose the larger opening, especially since I was unsure of the structure's soundness. I fought my way through briars and large branches to make a temporary pathway. I was glad I was still wearing waders, since they prevented many thorns from getting to my legs. I wondered how many patches the waders would need. I'd find out the next time I stepped into the water.

Finally I made it inside, then waited for my eyes to adjust to the dimness. As they did, I could see that at one time this place had been a getaway of sorts for someone. Fragments of old dishes and cups were littered about one corner; perhaps some kid wandering through the woods had stumbled across the cabin and either thrown them against the wall or used them as targets for his BB gun. I examined some of the shards and could see that they were from what were once nice pieces of pottery. A set of shelves still hung along one of the walls.

I found a set of stairs that ascended to an opening between two beams that ran the length of the cabin. The planks of pine boards that had been nailed to form a floor in the attic were still mostly intact. I was unsure about risking the stairs but found the first few boards surprisingly sturdy. Of course, that was the advantage of building stairs out of solid two-inch-thick pieces of oak. I cautiously climbed each riser one at a time. I stopped once my head was above the opening. The attic space was markedly darker than the main floor, and I could make out only a rough outline of the space. I wished I had a flashlight. I had one in the car, but I wasn't sure I was willing to venture up any farther even if I could see what was awaiting me.

The thought of the car drew me up short—I had completely forgotten about the time. I backed down the stairs more quickly than I should have, given that I didn't know how long they would hold, and read my watch: 12:15 P.M. "Damn," I said aloud as I hurried to the opening. This time I was far less careful as I pushed through the undergrowth. How long had Kelly been waiting? Retracing my steps toward the river, I located the small strip of red cloth I had tied to the bush under which I had hidden the sections of my rod. Quickly grabbing them, I turned to head back to the car when I heard a voice call "Cole!" It was Kelly.

I yelled, "Kelly, is that you?"

"Cole," the voice came back, "where are you?"

"Down by the creek." The tone in my voice probably gave a strong indication of my embarrassment, but as Kelly got closer, I saw he was smiling. I felt better knowing he wasn't irritated about my lateness.

As Kelly approached, he said, "Hey, is the fishing so good you couldn't tear yourself out of the water to meet me?" He was joking, but then he reached me and saw what I was holding. "What's with the rod?"

I glanced at the pieces in my hand and then back at him. "Uh, I was just getting ready to come up to meet you."

"How's the fishing been?" When I hesitated, Kelly continued. "Pretty great spot, huh!"

Now my reluctance to complain couldn't be hidden. "I don't want to disappoint you, but the fishing's been pretty lousy."

"Yeah, right," he said sarcastically.

"No, really. I fished this whole stretch for hours and managed to get only three small brookies to the net. Well, actually, to the hand. Using a net would have been a little bit of overkill for these fish."

"You're not kidding, are you?" Kelly now sounded genuinely surprised and even embarrassed.

"Hey, it's fine. Really. Who knows why they aren't feeding? That's fishing, isn't it—never any guarantees. If there were, we wouldn't do it." I wanted him to ease up on himself.

"Yeah, I know, but I've never had anything but great luck on this stretch of the Laurel."

He was gazing at the water behind me as if he were waiting for an explanation as to why his stream had fallen so short for his friend. I quickly changed the subject. "Kelly, can I ask you something? Do you know anything about the old cabin up on the ridge back there?" I thrust a thumb over my left shoulder.

"That thing? Yeah, I went up there once, but it was so overgrown I didn't waste my time looking around much."

"Do you know anything about who owned it?" My curiosity was piqued for some unknown reason.

"Nope. I've never talked with anyone who's even mentioned it. I've sure never asked about it."

"Hmm. Aren't you curious at all? I mean, I don't know how old it is, but it's in pretty good condition. I took a peek up the stairs into the—"

"You've been up there roaming around? No wonder you haven't caught any fish!"

"Ha, ha, ha." I was somewhat annoyed by his lack of interest and grabbed the chance to rib him some more. "Like I

said, the fishing was so lousy I had to find something to do."
The jab didn't offend him. "I'd like to get a flashlight from the
car and take a closer look around. What do you say?"

"Now let me get this straight. You travel fifteen hundred
miles to stand in one of the finest limestone creeks in central
Pennsylvania, a stream with the best brook trout fishing in a
hundred-mile radius, and you want to go exploring an old
run-down cabin in the woods? I don't get it."

"Oh, come on. Like I said, the fishing's been terrible, so
what do we have to lose?" His hesitation gave me a chance to
take charge. "Stay here, I'll be right back." But before I could
start heading up the hill to the car, he said, "Hang on, I'll
come with you and grab a light out of my trunk." Ah-ha, now
he was curious.

At the cars, we gently laid our rods in the trunk, grabbed
flashlights, and headed back down the rock and dirt path toward the cabin. Ten minutes later we were pushing our way
through the brambles where I had entered the cabin and soon
were inside. By now, the skies had cleared, and the bright sunshine caught the tan and brown colors of the interior sides of
the logs. Kelly walked to the corner where the dish fragments
were lying and began shuffling through them with his boots,
kicking them here and there in a sweeping motion. I inspected
the shelves and found pieces of newspaper stuck to the top,
obviously laid there long ago. I shone my flashlight on the
paper. In the upper right corner of the faded page was the date
July 21, 1948. "Hey, come look at this. There's an old paper
here from the 1940s."

Kelly walked over for a dutiful look. His tone revealed his
total lack of interest as he said, "Impressive." Yet in almost

the same instant, he stopped, squinted his eyes, and stared at the wall behind the shelf. "Hey, you still carry a knife?"

"Yeah, why?"

"Let me have it." I slipped the wader suspender off my right shoulder and slid my arm down into my jeans pocket to retrieve the knife, then handed it to him. He unfolded the blade and reached under the shelf to push it between the wall and the back edge of the shelf. Gently pushing the blade up, he muttered, "I'll be damned." He reached over the shelf and grabbed something so small I couldn't see it until he laid it in his hand.

"Holy shit, look at that," I said, stunned by what he had found.

I picked up the fly Kelly had eased out of its resting place and peered over the top of my glasses to study it. "Looks like about a size 14 Quill Gordon to me. What do you think?" I gently handed it back to him. "Give me the knife. Let me see if there are more." While I poked around behind the shelf, Kelly moved over to the window and examined the fly in the sunshine.

"Hey, you know, if you scraped off the rust, I think you could fish with this thing." Kelly, always the optimist.

I ran the knife blade down the length of the shelf but to no avail. I joined Kelly at the window for another look at the fly and stated the obvious. "Somebody who used this cabin fly fished down there in the Laurel." Kelly just smiled. I was eager to explore further and moved for the stairway. "Come on, let's look around upstairs." I began climbing the stairs, this time without reservation and with a new sense of purpose. When I reached the top step, I felt it sag beneath my weight. Easing back down one step, I put my hands up on the floor to test its strength. I slowly lifted myself to see if I could venture on. Seemed safe enough. Using both the floor and the step, I hopped up into the attic and sat on the edge, swinging my feet over the side. When Kelly was sure I wasn't going to come crashing through the ceiling, he joined me using the same maneuver.

We roamed around the attic. No, we tip-toed, because some boards bounced a bit as we moved over them. We agreed it would be smart to walk on the beams as much as we could. The only natural light creeping in came through small windows set on each side of the chimney. Through a set of metal grills framed into the floor, we could look down to the hearth below. A clever way to heat the attic space. I moved my flashlight toward the corner below one of the windows where I saw a pile of broken milled boards. After a few minutes of trying to put some of them together, I realized their purpose.

"Kelly, come look at this. I think this might have been a bed."

Shining his flashlight up and down the boards, he said, "I think you're right. The folks who used this must have slept up here to make more room downstairs."

"That explains the vent grates over here." I pointed to them with my light.

"Damn creative," he added.

As I moved my light across the wall space, I noticed that one of the logs had what looked like a door of some kind in it. Still wary of the floor, I grabbed one of the bed rails and used it to poke at the wall from about five feet away. Sure enough, the surface of the log was a door that swung back to the left, but just as I pulled it back, the door broke free and dropped to the floor. BAM! Kelly let out a yell that surprisingly didn't knock down any of the walls.

"What the hell was that?" he asked in a voice suitable for a Halloween outing.

"Look at this. There's a secret compartment over here in this log." I slowly edged over to it. We shone our lights into the space and could faintly make out what looked like a book. I reached in and grabbed it by the spine. After I blew off the dust and scraped away some of the spiderwebs, I could see that the book's cover was a marbled maroon-and-white pattern with triangles of leather covering each corner. The spine was of black leather and down it was written the word JOURNAL.

"What do you make of this?" I asked. Kelly moved closer to shine his light on the book, and I stuck my light under my arm and began thumbing through the pages. There was writing on almost every page. I bent back the front cover to find on the facing page, in large, bold printing, the title THE GENTLEMEN'S SOCIETY OF ANGLING. I looked at Kelly, and almost simultaneously we said, "Come on."

We bounded down the attic steps much faster than we probably should have, now ignoring our previous concerns about safety. It was as if we were kids again and had just found a pack of firecrackers in one of our dad's drawers. Kelly and I scrambled outside for better light by which to study the book. I turned to the second page and found writing done in a flowing script that long ago had disappeared from use. The ink had faded some, but the writing was still quite legible. I read it aloud.

The Sportsman's Creed

We, the undersigned, do solemnly bond ourselves to-gether this 25th day of September, 1933, to charter The Gentlemen's Society of Angling.

Be it resolved that we dedicate our interests to protect, defend, and commingle with the stream into which we venture in pursuit of the beautiful and mysterious trout. Believing that these communions replenish and strengthen the fiber of the soul, and as a means of sanctifying our common bond, we agree to abide by the beliefs set forth-with before us this day.

We do hereby pledge that:

1. We shall care for the river and its inhabitants as if they were our life-blood.

2. We shall take from the river only what will serve our needs of the moment.

3. We shall not during the times when The Society meets discuss or conduct any affairs beyond the purpose to which it is dedicated.

4. We shall, when necessary, determine when and whom shall be invited to become part of this brotherhood.

All this we do establish under the name—The Gentlemen's Society of Angling.

> *E. Fredrick Wheatley*
> *Julian Osgood*
> *Carlton Osgood*
> *Jackson Langsenkamp*
> *Barton J. Schoeppner*

The signatures at the bottom had been individually added by each of the members, though it appeared they were added at different times. I almost felt I was looking at some great, long-lost historic document.

I stood in stunned silence even after reading the entry an additional time. I closed the cover and scanned the woods as if I expected to find some explanation for this book I now held in my hand. Or perhaps I was afraid of being caught with something I wasn't supposed to have. Some parts of childhood never seem to leave us. I began wondering if the journal was original. By its condition and the faded ink on the pages, it would be hard to believe it wasn't. Besides, why would any-one go to this much trouble to forge such a record?

Kelly was more direct in expressing his thoughts. "Holy shit! Can you believe it?"

"Yeah." I had little to say. After a short pause I added, "What do you think we should do with it?" Kelly shrugged his shoulders, but his face and eyes reflected his thoughts. He was thinking the same thing I was—we both wanted to take the journal with us. "Do you think we should?" I asked.

Kelly responded exactly as I would have. "Who's going to know?"

Of course, he was right. Who was going to know we had the book? Obviously it had been in the wall of the cabin a long time. Although there was some evidence of insect dam-age, it was in surprisingly good condition.

As we walked back to the car, I asked, "Hey, what did you do with that fly?"

"Safe and sound, partner." He patted his front vest pocket.

That evening over dinner at Joe's Bar in Ligonier, Kelly, Lisa, and I talked about the journal and what we should do with it. As much as I wanted to claim "finder's-keeper's" rights, I knew the book should never leave the area that spawned it. To take it back to Colorado with me didn't seem right. We wondered if we should try to find relatives of one of the five signers and give the book to them.

After returning to Hawk Ridge, we found only one name in the phone book that matched—Langsenkamp. Kelly called and learned that this particular Langsenkamp family had moved to the area only two years ago and knew of no Jack Langsenkamp in the family tree. Kelly was irritated at how the people he phoned seemed annoyed that he had bothered them. "Typical ungrateful East Coasters," he sneered. Fine. This gave us the excuse to consider the book ours to do with as we pleased. After all, no one had come looking for it in all these years. Well, as far as we knew. We finally decided that Kelly would do some more checking around town to see if anyone had a lead on a relative. We were beginning to feel like Holmes and Watson with Miss Marple thrown in to add a twist. The one privilege I did claim was first dibs on reading it.

That night I settled into bed with the journal of The Gentlemen's Society of Angling. I was glad we'd wiped it clean. Sleeping with whatever had taken up residence with it in the cubbyhole over the years didn't seem appealing. I leaned back into the pillows propped up against the headboard and turned to the first entry.

> *God hath given much to man, but perhaps his greatest gift, the one which, by its very colors and existence signifies his ability to bring beauty to life, is the brook trout. Clearly, God fly fishes!*

I was struck by both the directness of the thought and the flare of the handwriting. This first entry obviously was penned by the same man who had inked in the creed on the previous page. The style of the "G" was unmistakable. I flipped to the end of the entry to find a name of the author. Nothing. I returned to the beginning and read on.

The most direct evidence of this is that his divine intervention placed in the soul of the brook trout the desire to rise to a fly. And any such creature, painted in the hues of summer and autumn, gilded with spots that iridesce in the sun, must also be allowed to reside in a place equally as spectacular. There can be none finer than Laurel Creek. Here, the "brookie" glides through water pure and freshened from the deep recesses of the earth. The nutrient-rich soil of the mountains is slowly added to the water as winter runoff rolls across the land to the river.

It is for these reasons that we band together to establish a residence along its banks. It is for these reasons that we seek to bring ourselves to these woods, a communion with all that is good and gentle about life.

Today is but one example of how we are changed by our presence in these environs. As I stepped into the cool mountain flow, the first cast full of anticipation, a good-sized fish nipped my LaBelle and surrendered himself to both the net and eventually the breakfast skillet. There is something exhilarating about setting a sun-up trout into a creel lined with blossoms of dew-covered mountain laurel. A taste of the cuisine leads one to believe that the fragrance of the bloom seeps its way into the flesh.

This being the first days of the cabin pleases me, and I'm sure the others, in ways that cannot be adequately

*expressed. Thus I, with sincere humility, do thank my
brethren for the opportunity to bask in the pleasures that
have been extended to us here, in this spot, by these waters. Here, surely, we touch the hand of the Almighty.*

October 2, 1933

The entry ended. There was no indication of authorship.
Just words. Magical words, too. Just as I had done with the
opening page, I reread the entry and tried to imagine the face
of the man who had written this piece. I thought back to
something my grandfather once told me. The life of every person you walk past or meet, no matter how common or unique,
is a story of triumph and tragedy. Even from reading one
entry, I sensed the entries would reveal some of the aspects of
these men's lives.

Doc

Yesterday we had our first fishing day with some of the kids from the county home. Even a few girls came along. We met the bus we'd borrowed from school at the Diamond, and then we all headed out to the cabin. I've never seen so much excitement. I think it was the first time some of the kids had been away from the home other than maybe for a Christmas visit with a local family.

Each of us, except for Bart, who stayed at the cabin to cook lunch for everyone, took kids to different parts of the stream. Although they were using only cane poles and worms, the kids were so excited just to be in the woods next to the water. Little is better in life than to hear the excitement in a child's voice when he yells, "I got one!" This usually is accompanied by some hopping and even a few screams of delight.

Lunch was accompanied by exaggerated stories of fish caught and lost. I admit I was concerned about how the kids from the county home would handle the day. I think it helped that our own kids were with them. For some of the kids, it was the first time they'd ever held a fishing pole.

None of us expected that watching the bus pull away to head back to Greensburg would hit us quite so hard.

The loneliness in the eyes of the faces pressed against the windows and the tiny hands waving good-bye struck deeply. The pent-up emotions flowed freely a week later as we read the simple but elegant thank-you letters the kids sent. Little Billy's last paragraph will always stick with me. "We pray every night that God will watch over us. He must have heard me since he let me visit your neat cabin and catch fish. Did he talk to you about this?"

It just breaks the heart.

July 21, 1949

"So, how high up were you when you jumped?" Doc Wheatley asked Corey as he layered more plaster gauze around the boy's calf.

"I was way up," a timid voice replied.

"Do you think anyone has ever been up that high, Corey?"

"Nope," he said with a sense of pride. "Even my big brother Larry was afraid to go up on that limb."

Doctor Wheatley told Corey to lie still while Nurse Ford finished applying the outer coat of plaster and it had dried. He turned his twinkling eyes toward Mrs. Burns. "He's probably going to have to wear the cast at least two months. We'll just have to see how quickly the bone heals. Since he's at an age when he's growing rapidly, we need to make sure the break heals properly. All we need is time and he'll be back up in those trees soon."

Mrs. Burns rolled her eyes over the tops of her glasses and said, "Not if I can help it."

Doc Wheatley turned to Corey, shrugged his shoulders, and smiled wryly. Corey returned the gesture.

While the final touches were put on the cast, Doc ruffled

Corey's hair, said good-bye to Mrs. Burns, and excused himself. He entered his office, took off his smock, and hung it on the coat tree standing in the corner. As he sank into his creased leather desk chair, he opened the file on his desk and jotted down notes about Corey's broken leg. After finishing the new entry, he flipped back in the file and read the notes he had made in the first entry. *Particularly difficult birth due to size of baby. Labor began at 7:00 A.M., delivery at about 11:00 A.M. next day. Significant loss of blood by mom. Iron supplement and water administered to stabilize fluid levels.* Doc tilted back in his chair and thought back to that day and many others like it. How many kids living in Ligonier had his hands helped into this world? Maybe someday he'd take time to count. But then again, he thought, what does it matter?

He reached for the phone and called Carol to let her know he'd be home in about a half hour. She reminded him about Barb's school program, and he assured her he would be home in plenty of time. As he hung up, he thought about how Corey wouldn't be attending the play. Doc hoped Corey didn't have a part in it. He didn't think so. Being in a play didn't seem to fit Corey. Doc turned off the lights and left the office, stopping briefly to let his nurse know he was leaving.

As he stepped outside, spring hit him squarely in the face. It wasn't merely the warm air or the sun still brightening the sky at 6:30 in the evening. It was also the patches of yellow daffodils planted many years ago by the Staffords, who once called his office their home. He was constantly amazed that the bulbs continued to produce flowers. How many years ago had they been set in the ground? At least six, since he had moved his office here to the Diamond more than five years ago.

The Diamond, as everyone in Ligonier called the town square, was a natural draw for Doc. There were always friendly faces and kind words. He often ate his lunch on one of the benches nestled against the flowers in the center area surrounded by the road. He didn't know why, but he particularly liked the uneven feel of the brick sidewalks; perhaps the earth beneath was trying to break out of its confinement. The view in any direction from the benches was of red brick one- and two-story buildings that rimmed the outer edge and gave the impression of safely enclosing the surroundings. The wall-to-wall buildings brought memories of his childhood in nearby Partington when he and his best friend Tom would guess how far around town they could walk on the rooftops.

Several businesses dotted the edge of the Diamond: Smitty's Hardware, The Stockade (which served the best steaks in town), Lulu's Beauty Salon, Osgood & Osgood Real Estate & Law, McKenzie's Clothiers. Although there weren't as many horse wagons as when he and Sally had moved to Ligonier, he was drawn to the ones that rolled through town periodically. The sound of hooves clomping on the brick pavers was more pleasant than the clanking of the Model As. Of course, someday there would be only cars. Progress? He headed for Jackson Street and home.

Doc had grown to know the regulars who hung around the Diamond. They could be found there even when the winter weather had driven most people to the shelter of their home fires. He first met Calvin on the Diamond. Calvin was an original—he had lived in Ligonier his entire life—and Doc had discussed fishing with him. The stories Cal told of the rivers and streams in the area set Doc on the path that eventually led to the arrangements to buy the land and the cabin on Laurel Creek. On one especially beautiful late spring day, Doc was so overcome by Cal's description of the abundant brook trout inhabiting the creek that he headed straight to Osgood & Osgood to take action.

As Doc entered the real estate firm, he was struck by the simplicity of the office. A secretary seated at a desk was centered directly in front of the entrance. To each side of her was a small office with a name painted on the frosted-glass windowpane. *Carlton Osgood. Julian Osgood.* Doc realized he wasn't fully comfortable with why he was there, but he had taken the first step and felt compelled to continue.

After he and Miss Medisch, the secretary, exchanged simple hellos, he said, "I'd like to talk with someone about whether there's any land for sale up in the highlands."

"If you'll have a seat right here, Doctor Wheatley, I'll see if Mr. Carlton or Mr. Julian can see you right now." She motioned to the waiting area, which held two boxy upholstered chairs.

As Miss Medisch rose and moved toward the offices, Doc at first thought it odd that she referred to them by their first names. The more he thought about it, however, he saw how it would be helpful, given that both men had the same last name. It was probably confusing when someone came in and asked for Mr. Osgood. Miss Medisch would have to ask whether the person wanted Mr. Carlton Osgood or Mr. Julian Osgood. So going by their first names was a sensible solution.

No sooner had Doc settled into a chair than a tall, muscular man approached with his hand extended. "Hello, Doctor Wheatley. I'm Carlton Osgood. Miss Medisch tells me you're interested in buying some land up in the Laurels. Would you like to step into my office so we can talk in private?"

As soon as Carlton Osgood said "buy some land," Doc Wheatley really began wondering why he was here. Showing Doc to a high-backed leather chair angled across the front of the desk, Carlton Osgood took his chair behind the desk and asked, "So, tell me what you're looking for."

"Well, I must admit that I'm here on sort of the spur of the moment. See, I've been talking with Cal. Do you know Cal?" Osgood assured him that everyone in town knew Cal. "Anyway, he's been telling me about the fishing up in Laurel Creek. I'm a fly fisherman, and I've fished some of the streams around here, but I hadn't been up to the Laurel until last week. Cal took me up there and I—well, I sort of fell in love with the area. I've been thinking about it ever since. So I guess I'm here to find out what it would take to own a little piece of that heaven."

As he paused, Carlton rose. "Doctor Wheatley, would you excuse me for just one minute? I'd like my brother Julian to join us. Do you mind?"

"No, not at all," Doc responded.

"I won't be a moment." A few seconds later the two brothers walked into Carlton's office. Doc rose to shake hands and exchange pleasantries with Julian and was taken by the resemblance between the two, although one distinctive feature was Julian's bald head. As Julian pulled up a chair opposite from Doc, Carlton began. "Julian, Doctor Wheatley was just inquiring about possibly buying some land up in the Laurels. He's a fly fisherman who has discovered, as he put it, 'a little bit of heaven' up there." As Carlton continued, Doc noticed

Julian's attitude markedly change. He had moved forward in his chair and was smiling broadly.

Julian asked the next questions. "Doctor Wheatley, what exactly are you intending to do with the land? Are you wanting to build a home or such?"

"Oh, goodness. I've haven't put one thought to something like that. Carol and I have a very comfortable home over on Jackson Street. Besides, I'm sure she'd have no desire to move that far out of town, and I couldn't be that far from my patients."

"So what are you wanting the land for?" Carlton asked.

"I guess I'd like to have a place where I could go fishing anytime I wanted. A place where I could throw up a tent for a few days and not worry about trespassing on somebody else's land. I've always dreamed about owning land with a trout stream running through it."

The more he talked, the more they smiled. He couldn't quite read the message behind their expression. He paused to get a sense of what was happening. The two Osgoods glanced at each other and then back to Doc.

Carlton said, "Doctor Wheatley, please forgive us for the way we're acting. You see, Julian and I are also fly fishermen."

Suddenly Doc realized what the smiles meant. The Osgoods weren't thinking about a big sale or a new client as much as they were thinking about fishing. At that moment, the conversation shifted exclusively to fishing. They discussed the various spots where Doc had fished and gave him several suggestions of new places he could go. Then they began sharing ideas on favorite flies and when was the best time to use them. The more the Osgoods talked, the more Doc warmed to them. Finally, he looked at his watch and realized he should have been back at the office some time ago.

"Oh, Lord, I need to get back to the office," he said, suddenly rising from his chair.

"Doctor Wheatley," Julian began, "I am so sorry. We completely got away from why you came to see us in the first place. It's not very often we run into a fellow fly fisherman. We know plenty of bait fishermen, but fly fishermen are hard to come by in this town." As they walked Doc to the door, Julian continued. "If it's all right with you, Carlton and I will do a little scouting around up along the Laurel Ridge and see if there's any land available. Offhand, I can't think of anyone who's mentioned wanting to sell some land, but that doesn't mean such people aren't around. As with many things in life, sometimes you have to ask."

Saying good-bye with a handshake, Doc exited and began walking around the Diamond toward his office. He wasn't thinking about the possibility of buying land but instead was wondering if he could find any of the fishing spots the Osgoods had mentioned.

His wonderment faded the next afternoon when Julian stopped by his office. Did he want to go fishing with them on Saturday? They wanted to take him up to Laurel Creek. It seemed they had a friend who let them access the creek from his property, and he might know if anyone had an interest in selling land. How could Doc turn down the invitation?

When Saturday arrived, Julian and Carlton picked him up, and they headed out of town toward the mountains. As they drove along, not once was the topic of buying land mentioned. It seemed to Doc that the purpose of the day was fishing, not business. That suited him just fine. Since leaving the Osgoods's office, he hadn't given any thought at all to what he had originally gone to see them about.

Finally, Carlton turned the truck onto a gravel road leading into the trees. Eventually, they stopped in front of a small home whose owner certainly took pride in his abode. The house was meticulously painted and was surrounded by a stunning array of morning glories, pansies, and peonies. It's a picture postcard, Doc thought. Carlton honked the horn a couple of short beeps, and the three men piled out the sides of the truck. They heard the front screen door slam, and a short, thick man about their own age walked rapidly toward them waving. He was wearing a pair of bib overalls that looked well used and also comfortable around his barrel chest and middle torso.

"Doc, this is Walt Hazlett. Walt, Doc Wheatley," Julian said.

"Pleasure," Walt said as they shook hands. "So, you boys gonna do some fishing, huh? Well, the creek finally cleared after last week's rain, so those little buggers ought to be ready for some action." Doc liked the sound of that. They continued exchanging comments about the fishing possibilities. Doc had been quiet up to that point but finally chimed in with a compliment about Walt's place. "Thanks. The wife's the one who takes care of the flowers and stuff. That's all her idea. My job's keeping the paint on the walls," he added with a laugh.

While they were assembling their gear, Carlton asked Walt if he knew of anyone who was interested in selling some land in the area. He didn't say it was Doc who was interested. Walt paused, then said, "I sure haven't heard anything, but then folks up here don't ask a lot of questions about other people's business. I'll keep my ears open, and if anything turns up, I'll let you know. I wish I could join you boys, but I have to go over to Bessie Johnson's place and take a look at her roof. She says the roof's leaking. Well, you boys enjoy yourselves. Doc, it was a pleasure."

With that Walt headed toward his truck, fired up the engine, and drove off. On the walk down to the stream, Doc learned that Walt was the best carpenter and mason in the area. The Osgoods always recommended him if a house needed work before it sold. Doc now understood the overalls and the roughness of the hand he had shaken. As they walked on, Doc swore he could begin smelling the water.

When they arrived at the water's edge, Doc began rummaging through his fly billfold in search of something small and pale yellow. He had noticed several similar insects fluttering among the bushes and reeds that graced the bank. He finally settled on a size 16 Bright Fox. As he was about to step into the water, Doc noticed Carlton and Julian. The brothers were standing erect, shoulder to shoulder, each with a flask held chest-high in front of him. Just as Doc was about to speak, they bowed their heads gently toward the water and took a quick hit from the flasks. Carlton chuckled as he saw Doc's puzzled expression. "Toasting the river gods," he said. "Care for a snort?" Doc hesitated but took a drink. This was the first of many oddities Doc would come to appreciate about the Osgoods. "Let's get to it," Carlton added as he tucked the flask into his shirt pocket. "What did you tie on, Doc?"

"A Bright Fox." Doc leaned over to show them.

"Damn good choice. Okay, Doc," Julian said with a hand pointing upstream, "if you'll take this path upstream a hundred yards or so, you'll see a great little pool stuffed with fish. I'm going in here, and Carlton's heading downstream. No sense falling over each other with all this water around. Sound good?"

There was little Doc could say. He had no idea where to fish other than it needed to be in the water. Ready to head off, he stopped and walked over to Julian. "How about one more for good luck?"

"Doc, I knew I was going to like you." Julian passed him the flask.

The farther upstream he walked, the more enchanted Doc became. The creek cut a twenty-yard-wide swath through the mix of hardwoods and hemlock. The path he followed was barely discernible as it wove its way through the thick undergrowth of ferns and laurel. Estimating he had gone about the right distance, he began looking for the pool. He noticed a spot where the water darkened and smoothed that indicated a deepening of the bottom. This must be the pool. The only way to fish it was from a midstream gravel bar, and the only way to get there was to wade in below the bar and walk up. As he retraced his steps, he tried to find a place where the brush thinned and he might squeeze through. Suddenly, he realized he was almost back to where Julian was fishing. Turning back upstream, he wondered about finding access above the pool but decided the likelihood was remote. Finally, he decided he must just shove his way through the dense thicket.

Within a few steps, he regretted having already strung his rod. Every movement deeper into the bushes resulted in a need to free his line from a branch. He tried lifting his rod above the bushes only to have the tip scrape on the overhead branches of the tree behind him. He lowered the rod, then let out a short gasp and ducked when he was startled by a sudden movement directly above him. He looked up and caught a brief glimpse of two great-horned owls flying across the stream into the trees. A voice from downstream yelled, "Hey, did you see those?"

Doc felt trapped. The brush he had squeezed through had sprung back together to enclose him. He laughed and pressed resolutely forward toward the water only a few feet ahead. His line was tangled in the brush again. He found his fly, dislodged it from a stick, bit it off the tippet, and reeled in his line. Then he turned around to back toward the water, holding his rod out in front of him. Eventually, his left boot started slipping down the bank. A second later it hit solid rock only a few inches below the surface of the water. He felt lucky he wasn't neck deep. He carefully backed up until he was completely free of the brush and could raise his rod. He shook his head in amazement. It must have taken him ten minutes to walk five feet.

After catching his breath, he examined his rod for damage. All looked fine. Wading out to the middle of the stream, he could see Julian's rod tip bending toward the water over the tops of the bushes. He muttered aloud to himself, "Wonder how many fish he's caught and I haven't even put out a cast?"

Yet when he finally reached the bar and had restrung his rod, the bushes seemed in the distant past. The pool was teeming with fish. Rises pocked the surface everywhere as fish sipped bugs off the surface. Doc was so eager to start fishing, he skipped an eye on the rod and had to restring it again. As he prepared for his first cast, he wished he could see below the surface. The telltale rings on the water sent his imagination vaulting.

Doc worked out line, finally setting the fly on the water at the head of the pool. He wondered if the fish could tell the difference between his puff of feathers and the real thing. A few seconds later he set the hook. Instantly the other rises stopped as the splashing fish alerted the rest to danger. He gently brought the fish, a nice ten-inch brookie, to the net and nestled it into the wet leaves he had spread across the bottom of his creel. Again and again, he let the pool calm, careful not to recast until the rises began anew. Starting with his fifth catch, he began returning the fish to the water. Four were enough for lunch.

He worked the pool through the morning until he heard a whistle from downstream. He assumed it and the high sun signaled lunch. Doc suppressed the just-one-more-cast urge and went to meet his friends. Not wanting to face the bushes again, he waded in the stream until he found an opening along the bank. He could smell a wood fire.

Doc knew the contented look on his face told the Osgoods he had had a successful morning. They noticed the scratches across his arms and neck. "Doc, if you don't mind my asking, what the hell happened to you? You look like you've been in a fight," Julian said.

"Well, the bushes won the battle, but I won the fishing war." He opened his creel and set it down next to the fire. "When you guys finish frying those, can I toss these in?"

As he settled in next to the fire, the three fly fishermen exchanged stories about the morning. The flask was passed a few times too. Eventually, Doc told the Osgoods about growing up in northeastern Pennsylvania and playing hooky to fish in the Poconos. It was there that his uncle had introduced him to fly fishing. It wasn't until he finished medical school that he was able to start fishing again, though he did take some time to fish with a school chum. He had even made it up to New York once.

The rest of the afternoon, they fished close enough together that they could talk between catches. Near dusk they headed for the truck. After a while, Doc again brought up the idea of owning some land. "Can you imagine having a place of your own up here? A place you could really get to know?" There was no need to respond.

On an early summer day, Carlton stopped by Doc's office with news. "Doc, you might want to sit down while I tell you this. Walt Hazlett just left my office and told me he had heard about a place that might be for sale. It seems ten or so years ago, a bootlegger had a still up on Steiner Ridge, and the revenuers finally got wind of his operation and shut him down. Apparently the guy was a relative of the marshal over in Latrobe, and he was able to work out a deal with the feds that if he stopped moonshining and left the area, they wouldn't prosecute him. Anyway, Walt said the property has been transferred to the town fathers in Latrobe and they might want to unload it. There's even a cabin on the property. Now, here's the best part. The guy needed water, right? Guess where he got it?" Carlton paused. "The Laurel runs right through the property."

Doc couldn't believe this luck. "How much do they want for it?" The moment the words were out, he realized he was second-guessing himself. He hadn't even seen the place. The pictures in his mind overtook him.

"Doc, Julian and I would be happy to go up there for you, but we wondered if you'd want to go with us?"

"When are you going? I've got patients coming in all day. Also, Jessie Baker's baby's due any day now, and I'd sure hate to be off looking at some bootlegger's cabin and have her go into labor." Doc wondered if he was reaching for excuses.

"Look, Doc, there's no hurry. The land's been unoccupied for several years. Somehow I can't imagine there's a horde of people headed up there to look at it." Carlton studied Doc carefully. "Tell you what. What say we wait until Jessie's baby is here and you can find a day that will work for you. Sound okay?"

There was no way to refuse. Doc agreed and stood up, then realized Carlton had more to say and sat down again. "Is there more?"

"Yes." Carlton's voice had a marked firmness. This alarmed Doc, but he couldn't guess the cause for the change. "Doc, this is sort of awkward for me to ask, so I'm just going to say it." He drew a breath. "Julian and I wondered if you'd be interested in having some partners in buying this land. We've been talking and thought that if we all pooled our resources, maybe we could go in on this together."

Partners? Doc heard the word echo in his head. Partners? "Well, to be frank, I hadn't put a thought to it." He sat quietly for a moment, then rose and moved to the window to look out the back of his office. He spun around in time to see Carlton about to speak again and looked straight at him. "You know, Carlton, it might make this whole crazy idea a little easier for Carol to swallow."

Carlton seemed to like Doc's response. "Look, think about it. Okay? I better go. When you're ready to head up to look the place over, give us a nod."

Two weeks later, the three men found themselves once again in the truck heading out of town. The conversation was relatively light, given the nature of the jaunt. They went over the moonshiner's story a few times. Julian added that he had talked to the records clerk in Greensburg and learned that the property might be had for a few dollars per acre. Just how many dollars was the concern. The clerk was figuring out the total and said he would have the figures ready in a week or so. He also said the sale would have to be approved by the county aldermen.

Once they arrived in the general area, they pulled the truck to the side of the road. The only directions they had were that the cabin was about four miles up the left fork of a dirt road that they could pick up on the east side of the main road between Latrobe and Ligonier. They all agreed that was as clear as molasses. But then again, this was a moonshiner's place, and such operations weren't typically located in convenient spots. This realization made the place even more appealing.

Finding the cabin was a little easier after they stopped and asked a local farmer hoeing a field if he knew the whereabouts of a cabin up in the mountains. His wariness was clear when he bluntly asked, "Who wants to know?" Once they convinced him they weren't government men but were fishermen, he exhibited a slight increase in hospitality. The best clue he gave them was to look for a large oak that had been chopped in half after it fell across the road. They hoped the truck was now parked next to this very tree.

The three of them split up to cover more area but first agreed that they'd signal with a whistle if the cabin was spotted. Several minutes later, Doc found a loosely stacked pile of firewood. As he approached the pile, he noticed the cabin farther up the ridge and whistled for the Osgoods to join him. After a couple of directional checks with yells, the three of them stood looking at the moonshiner's cabin. It was set in a grove of oak and beech trees that formed a soft, green canopy. The ground was covered with ferns and rhododendrons and spindly saplings grasping for sunlight that couldn't reach the forest floor. The smashed remnants of the still, including its tubing and a large boiling vat, were strewn around the area. The fed-boys' axes had definitely done their damage.

Mud and limestone had been used as chinking between the graying hand-shaved logs. The log walls sat atop a foot-high foundation of fieldstone and mortar. A window was centered on each of the three walls except the one where the chimney stood.

After peering into the windows, Julian spoke first. "Hey, this place looks all right. Let's take a look inside." He walked to the door and tried the latch.

They estimated the single room to be about twenty by thirty feet, and stairs along one wall led to a second floor. While Doc and Julian kicked through the clutter on the floor, Julian went upstairs. There he found a rough-hewn, plank floor with empty burlap grain bags tossed into a corner. Several mice scurried across the floor when Julian rooted a boot into the bags. Joining the others downstairs, he asked, "So, what do you think?"

Doc answered, "The place looks in pretty good shape. Some of the chinking needs work, but that's no big deal. How's the upstairs?"

"The floor's solid, and I didn't see any sign of leaks," Julian said. "What about the fireplace?"

Carlton looked at his brother. "No problems as far as I can tell, though it looks like raccoons have moved in."

Once outside again, they roamed around the cabin poking and kicking until they were all satisfied the building was structurally sound. It was better than they had hoped it would be.

Next, they walked a few hundred feet down to the creek to check out the prospects. Their excitement over the cabin only grew when they saw the stretch of water.

"How much land is there?" Doc asked as he gazed at the large rocks behind which he knew there were fish holding.

"I think the guy said about five acres," Carlton answered.

"Is it all on this side of the water?"

"I don't know," Carlton offered. "I'm sure it goes to the creek from this side. That's all we'd need, isn't it?" The question drew chuckles from the other two. After one more look through the cabin, they roamed the woods before heading back to the truck.

A week later, the three of them met to examine the letter Carlton had received from the Greensburg county clerk's office. It explained that the property contained just under nine acres stretching from the road to the creek. Unpaid taxes for the past six years amounted to $877. Carlton said it would be necessary to file several deed applications with the county and have the sale approved, but generally, it was a straightforward transaction. A possible concern, however, was that the county had to post a public notice about the intent to sell, as well as notify any living relatives. If anyone stepped forward to challenge the sale, it could be delayed several weeks or months. The good news was that in six years, theirs had been the only inquiry about the property.

"So, even though we'll have to wait for everything to clear, I think it's ours if we want it," Carlton concluded. "Personally, I think we'd be crazy to pass this up." The decision was made.

Two weeks later, they made the drive to Greensburg and signed the papers. Julian arranged for Walt Hazlett to give the cabin a once-over and dig a privy. A week later, Doc, Julian, and Carlton arrived at the cabin for their first weekend and toasted the day with a glass of MacCallan's. After several hours arranging some meager provisions and furniture the Osgoods had picked up through their business, they spent the afternoon fishing.

As dusk settled into the trees, Doc brought out a book to the campfire and handed it to Julian. "Guys, I'd like to make a proposal. I think we should have a name for our group. I've been thinking about this some and suggest we name ourselves The Gentlemen's Society of Angling. What do you think?"

Carlton and Julian looked at each other. Carlton said, "A little pretentious, don't you think?"

Doc smiled. "Read what I wrote, and if you agree, sign your name," he said.

They read the creed, then Carlton silently reached over for the pen Doc extended his way. Both Osgoods signed under the creed Doc had written, then Julian handed the book back to Doc. "Doc, we left room for your name above ours. It's only fitting since all this was your idea."

Doc cocked his head to the right a little. "This is too good to be true." He opened the book and inscribed his name. That night he set down his first entry on the page following the creed with the signatures.

Having just spent the first night in the cabin, I must admit that although the solitude was enjoyable, it was not the same as being alone. It makes me wonder if there is more here than merely the chance to fish and get away from the world. Despite the occasional disagreements about what we should do to the cabin, or how we should handle bringing friends for a day or so, there is an unspoken level of communication that binds us together. I came to realize that as I sat here, alone, next to the Laurel.

All along this stream are memories that hold fixed in place despite the movement of the water. Human moments cannot be washed away. Should people ever want to know, I could walk them into the water or woods and show them where a first fish was caught, where a slight slip on a rock resulted in a complete dunking, where a rod tip was broken after a little too much drink, where. . . . Yet even that doesn't complete the picture. There's much more here than that.

The Osgoods

Doc said that this journal is for everyone to write in, so Julian and I will make our first entry. This cabin idea has been the greatest. Lately, we've spent more time here than we have at the office. But, then again, it is spring!

We tried some new spots today upstream from the cabin. Julian discovered a nice pool just above a little rock shelf that held some really nice trout. We both decided to try some new flies. I even got Julian to try a floating fly rather than his typical Woods he drags through the water. It took him a while to spot the takes, but he managed to get the job done.

This afternoon, we decided it was too nice to spend the evening in the cabin, so we began arranging some logs around a fire pit we dug at the center of three beech trees that form a nice triangle. We had to do some chopping to fit the logs between the trunks. I think Doc will like what we've done. Should be a great place to tell and listen to a few lies.

So, as we light the fire, we pour our first drinks of the evening and say thanks, Doc, for all this. It was your idea, and we are grateful to get to tag along on the journey. Sköal!

Carlton, May 16, 1934

Sliding a chair up under the plank table in the middle of the room to eat some breakfast, Doc looked at Jack and said drily, "Those two have screws loose."

Jack Langsenkamp's weary eyes smiled from behind his coffee cup. "They're harmless. Besides, they're great entertainment." He took a sip and added, "Surely you don't buy the story about Howling Wolf, do you?"

Doc's response seemed to get to the heart of the matter. "I don't think it matters what any of us think. They believe it. And I'm damn sure anything we say won't change them." He paused to take a bite of toast. "Can't you just see those two in their Boy Scout uniforms, painted up, sitting with some old Indian named Howling Wolf?"

Although Julian and Carlton had conducted their howling ceremony at different spots around the woods, the full story of Howling Wolf didn't come forth until after The Society's other members had chased them down from the roof. It was evening the next day that Julian and Carlton had spun the tale around the campfire.

"Geez, we'd been planning the trip for over a year," Julian began. "And when the day came for us to catch the train to Pittsburgh, you'd have thought we were going to see Blackjack Pershing himself to volunteer for the AEF. We had packs, tents, rifles, everything. Besides Carlton and our dad, there were Lyle Smythe and Pudgy Brizendine. Carlton, remember that gunnysack Pudgy wouldn't let out of his sight?" Carlton nodded. "Our pal Pudgy had this sack full of food his mom had given him in case he got hungry on the train." Julian paused. "Anyway, Scout Troop 78 was bound for the Dakota Black Hills."

Carlton jumped in. "Julian, remember that second day out of Chicago when we started smelling that God-awful stink in the train car? Pudgy had stuck a piece of cheese in his sack, and after three days under his seat, well, you can imagine. Somewhere west of Sioux Falls, the coyotes found a gift from the prairie gods." He mimicked tossing the sack out a window while pinching his nose between his fingers. He and Julian laughed hysterically. "I hope it didn't kill any of them.

"We reached Rapid City sometime in the morning, and let me tell you, I was ready to get off that train. The depot wasn't at all what I expected. The building was only about the size of this cabin with the main line and a pull-off running alongside. When that train left, there was no one around but the five of us, the depot guy, and a farmer picking up a Sears-Roebuck order. We could see town about a quarter mile behind the depot, so we began walking that way with our gear. Julian, remember that town?"

Julian stood and poured himself another glass of Mac-Callan's. Grabbing a stick to stir the fire, he continued. "Yeah, there were maybe fifteen or twenty buildings—a small boarding house, a general store, some houses, a church. But the main thing was the sawmill on the south end of town. The mill dwarfed all other buildings in the town. Logs were stacked as far as the eye could see, it seemed. Teams of Belgians were dragging the logs in one end of the building, while other teams hauled wagons of boards out the other end. The air was filled with sawdust mixed with steam, and the buzz of the saws drowned out all other sounds. Dad had to yell to be heard above the noise. But the best part was the mountains to the west. The Black Hills. Did you know that the Black Hills are the most sacred piece of earth to the Sioux? They call them Paha Sapa.

"Once we got into town, we headed to the general store, where Dad told us kids to wait on the sidewalk. So we stood shuffling our feet along the wooden planks of the walkway watching the horses and wagons loping up and down the street. I remember something Pudgy said while we were waiting. He wondered where all these people lived, since there were a whole lot more of them than houses. About then, Dad came out of the store and called us over to him. He said, 'Boys, I need to go down to the livery and see if there's a way for us to get out to Pedersen's farm. The store owner has a brother with a farm a few miles out of town and said we could probably camp there. I want you to stay here until I get back.'"

By now, Julian had resumed his seat next to his brother. Taking another swig of whiskey, he continued. "Shortly after Dad left, we got our first real exposure to the West. Carlton and I were sitting on our packs resting up against the wall of the store when he gave me a hard nudge in the side and told me to look down the street. I did and saw my first real Indian. You could tell he was an Indian because he had long braids, even though his hair was gray, hanging down each side of his face. His clothes were pretty much like everyone else's, but he was definitely an Indian. Part of me wanted to jump up and talk to him, but another part of me was too scared to act. The scared part won. That Indian turned up the steps and headed right into the general store. As he passed us, he tilted his head back a little, gave us a serious look, and nodded his head—almost as if he was sizing us up or something. Remember that, Carlton?"

"Do I ever!" Carlton's voice rang with a kid's excitement. The other Society members knew they were in for a long story. "You'd have thought we'd have been scared, the way he looked at us. But I remember it wasn't like that. It was almost as if he was acknowledging us with a hello or something. After he went in the store, we all started talking about who he was and what kind of Indian he was. Pudgy wondered if he was going to scalp us. Of course, we played along and told Pudgy the Indian was a great warrior because he had long braids and only Indians who had killed many soldiers could wear his hair long." Carlton began to laugh again. "Pudgy was so scared he went around the corner of the store and wouldn't come out until Dad returned.

"As soon as we saw Dad, we ran up to him and told him all about the Indian. Dad had to go around the store and convince Pudgy that Indians didn't kill people anymore. After we had all that settled, everyone went inside and grabbed the supplies Dad had bought—flour, some salted meat, and a large sack of beans. But we didn't see the Indian." He paused to let the comment settle in a little. "It was as if he had disappeared." He paused again. "Then Lyle told Pudgy the beans were for him so he could keep the bears away at night." This brought a huge laugh from Julian.

Doc interrupted. "Seems to me you were pretty tough on this Pudgy guy. Did he ever get tired of your crap and just haul off and slug you?"

Carlton smiled. "Nah, Pudge loved it. He knew we were kidding, though we could get his goat pretty easily." He looked at Julian and softly laughed. "Anyway, we grabbed all the food and followed Dad down the street and around a corner to a corral that held several horses. Dad told us to drop our stuff against the fence but to make sure not to put it close enough for the horses to reach it. He said we were going to have to spend the night beside the corral, and in the morning we'd head out to where we were going to camp. Apparently the guy who owned the farm was due in town the next day, and if we were lucky, we could get a ride with him out to the mountains. So we set up the tents under a big old oak tree. The rest of the day, we were free to roam the town, as long as we didn't go near the sawmill. Sometime about dusk, we got a fire going and cooked some beans and salt pork. While we ate, we watched the mill guys bring all the horses over to the barn where they got washed and fed and put in their stalls for the night.

"The next day, we woke to the sounds of the steam engines firing up in the sawmill. While we folded up our tents, the big Belgians were harnessed into teams and driven to the mill. Later that morning, the farmer showed up, and Dad talked to him about hauling our gear. The problem was that not all of us could fit into the wagon because of the supplies he was picking up, and we had to take turns walking and riding out to his place. It was a long hard walk, especially for Pudgy.

"The farm sat at the back end of a valley with the pine-covered hills circling around it on three sides. As we unloaded our gear from the wagon, Dad and Mr. Pedersen started talking about spots where we could camp. We circled around them listening just when our biggest surprise yet came walking out of the barn. It was the Indian we had seen in town. Pedersen called him over to meet Dad. 'Mr. Osgood, this is Jess Unger. Jess, these boys are from back East and want to see our beautiful Black Hills.' He turned back to Dad. 'If anyone knows where to go, it's Jess. He's spent many years in the hills.' Well, you can imagine what was going through our minds. Here we were standing right next to a real Indian. Pudgy hid behind Dad.

"Dad had us begin assembling our packs and told us to divide up the supplies so everyone carried his share of the load. The three men began talking among themselves. When we kids were about done, Dad came over and told us to finish up because we were headed out right away. The men had decided that Jess Unger should take us into the hills, but he needed to get back to the farm before dark, so there was no time to waste. So the five of us and our Indian guide headed into the Paha Sapa." It was obvious to everyone around the campfire that Carlton had used the Sioux name for dramatic purposes. It hadn't worked.

Julian picked up the story. "We must have walked for two hours, climbing and climbing into the hills. Finally, we crested a hill and started a descent toward a valley we could see over the tops of the trees. A short time later, we reached a small lake where we made our camp. Jess said the lake was known as Greasy Grass. He made some final arrangements with Dad and headed back up the slope and into the trees. We were going to camp at the lake for four days and then head back out."

By now, Jack, Doc, and Bart weren't seeing any connection between the Osgoods's story and the howling ceremony, and they shifted restlessly on their log seats. Sensing their impatience, Julian got to the point. "For the first two days, we did some hunting and fishing and swimming, but mostly we just walked in the woods. Just after dusk on the third night, things really changed. We were sitting around the campfire and watching the moon crest the hills to the south. Pudgy was the first to hear an animal cry from higher up in the trees. He told everyone to be quiet. At first we didn't hear anything, but suddenly, there was a howl that echoed across the lake and into the trees behind us. We were all a little scared. After hearing it again, we turned to Dad for an answer. He said it was probably just a coyote and there was nothing to worry about as long as the fire was going. Of course, Pudgy and Carlton immediately grabbed some more logs and tossed them on the fire." Julian grinned at his brother. Carlton shook his head from side to side in disagreement. "The best part, though, was when Lyle began asking Dad about bears and wolves and what-not. That really got us going. Even though Dad said all the bears and wolves had been killed, we didn't believe him. Anyway, before you know it, we have a roaring fire, and the howling stops. Just when we think we've scared off whatever it was, the howling starts again—only this time it's closer to us. Oh, boy, you should have seen us then. We started asking about getting rifles ready. By now, even Dad was getting worried.

"A few minutes later, we started hearing noises in the trees as if something was moving toward us. Well, Dad told us all to get in his tent, and he grabbed his gun and shoved a couple of loads into the chamber. We got in the tent and stuck our heads out the flap to watch what was happening. The moon was so bright we could see into the trees pretty well. Lyle kept saying he saw a big animal moving in the trees. Of course, then we all started seeing things. For what seemed like hours but was probably just a few minutes, everything was dead silence—no howling, no brush noise, nothing." Julian had scooted himself up to the front of the log he was sitting on, pretending he was holding a tent open with his hands. "The next sound we hear is . . ." Julian paused for a moment. 'Osgood, it's me, Jess Unger.'

"We kids took what seemed to be our first breath in hours and bolted out of the tent. Jess had a bedroll slung across his back, and he and Dad were standing next to the fire talking. Lyle ran up and asked if Jess had heard the wolf. Jess laughed and said, 'Boys, there are no more wolves in the Black Hills. They were killed off years ago when the first gold miners invaded the area.'" Julian paused, then said, "I recall it clearly because Jess had a real tone of sadness in his voice. Remember that, Carlton?"

Carlton nodded his head and spoke. "Yeah, he seemed to be recalling something painful. Anyway, Jess told us he had come out to see if we were okay. Dad invited him to sit down, and within seconds, Lyle was badgering him about the howling we had heard. Jess began laughing again. 'Oh, that. I know exactly what that was.' Suddenly, he put a hand up next to his mouth and let out a howl that nearly knocked Pudgy off his seat. Everyone was stunned. 'You mean that was you we heard?' Dad asked him. Jess just nodded. Eventually, we all laughed a little and settled in around the fire. After Dad brought Jess a cup of coffee and some food, Jess began asking us about where we were from. But we wanted to hear about being an Indian, and that was when Jess Unger told us his story.

"Boys, I have two names, the one you know already, and Sunkmanituwaho, which means Howling Wolf. My mother was an Oglala Sioux. My father was a prospector named Jedediah Unger. The name I go by, Jess Unger, is the name my

father gave me. My mother gave me my Sioux name one summer during the Moon of Chokecherries when I was about your age. It must be at least fifty years ago that my father found my mother, almost dead, in the hills.

"During the Great War for the Black Hills, my mother's tribe was constantly fleeing the soldiers so they wouldn't be forced out of the Paha Sapa and onto reservations in the south. My mother, who was a young woman at the time, got separated from her family while she was out gathering food. It seems that while she was wandering the hillsides, a scout returned to camp and informed everyone that soldiers were coming. Within minutes, the entire group was on the move to escape the army. It wasn't until she returned to what had been the camp that she discovered she had been left behind. She tried to follow the tribe's tracks but realized that it was an almost hopeless cause. She knew better than to follow the tracks of the army horses for fear she'd be captured. Sadly, my mother never located her tribe, and she wandered in the Paha Sapa for weeks living on only the berries and the occasional rabbit she could trap.

"Sometime during those weeks, she ran into my father, who was digging for gold in a remote area of the hills. Weak and afraid, she tried to flee but couldn't. It turned out that my father took care of my mother, giving her food and shelter. Over time, he earned her trust. After a while, my father learned that my mother's people had been captured by General Crook and moved to a reservation. My mother was torn about what to do. She knew if she turned herself in she would be sent to a reservation somewhere, but there was no guarantee it would be where her people were. She also knew that the

man who had saved her was the reason the Sioux had to be re-
moved from the Black Hills. You see, the trail that had been
cut for the army was called Thieves Road because it was the
main entry into the hills for the gold miners. Yet he was also
the reason she was alive, and she had found him to be an hon-
orable and gentle man. Eventually, my father persuaded her to
stay with him, and they established a common-law marriage.
A few years later, I was born."

Carlton took a break from Unger's story to pour a drink.
The tale The Society members had assumed to be a hoax perpetrated by the Osgood brothers now had everyone at the
cabin drawn in. It was as if they were all back in the Black
Hills sitting around the fire listening to Howling Wolf.

"The whole time I was growing up, my parents raised me
to live in my dad's world. However, whenever my dad was
away in the hills or had to go to the assay office, my mother
told me stories about her tribe and the wars between the Sioux
and the army. One late summer, my mother took me with her
into the hills to collect chokecherries. She always knew when
they were ripe by waiting until the fourth moon appeared.
This is why it is known as the Moon of the Chokecherries.
While we were gathering berries, we heard a moan coming
from a small cave. We entered the cave, and the moaning
changed to a growl. We backed out, and a wolf came creeping
after us. Once my mother and I were in the sunlight, we saw
the wolf appear at the opening. The wolf was the saddest-
looking animal I had ever seen. It was very old with matted
fur and spots where the fur was completely missing. When it

bared its teeth at us, we could see that some of them were missing or broken. This animal was near death.

"My mother told me this must be the last wolf in the Black Hills and that it was a sign. We stood still and watched the old wolf. Chasing us out of the cave had used up nearly all its strength, and it sank slowly to its haunches. My mother began speaking to it in Sioux, and soon the wolf's ears stood up as if the animal was listening to her. Its eyes brightened. When she finished, I asked her what she had said. She explained that she told the wolf she had also lost her people. As I watched what had once been a great animal that roamed the Paha Sapa as a king, I could see the sadness return to its eyes. Then the wolf mustered what little strength it had and howled the most mournful plea I have ever heard. My mother grabbed my arm and begged me to follow her. As we walked away, I glanced back and watched the wolf turn and head back into the cave. My mother and I talked very little the rest of the day.

"Later that afternoon as we sat around the table in our cabin, she explained to me that the wolf had been sent by the Great Spirit for me. She said that in each child's life, a guardian spirit is picked from among the animals and appears to that person and serves as a lifelong companion. For her it was an elk. From underneath her blouse she took a small leather bag, reached into it, and pulled out a tip of antler. She explained that by carrying it with her, she was always surrounded by her guardian spirit. She said the wolf had been sent for me.

"A few weeks later, I went into the hills alone to the cave where we had seen the wolf. When I got there, I heard no sound, so I crawled into the cave only to find it empty. There was no sign of the wolf other than some tufts of fur and some *rabbit bones piled up against a wall. Among the bones I found several teeth that could have come only from the wolf. I gathered these up and wrapped them in some of the fur. I returned home with the teeth and fur and showed them to my mother. That was when she gave me my Sioux name, Sunkmanituwaho. Howling Wolf."*

Carlton fell silent. Julian resumed the story in a soft whisper. "Sunkmanituwaho. Howling Wolf. We kids were completely transfixed by Jess's story and kept repeating his Sioux name aloud. Then Jess pulled a leather cord from around his neck and opened an amulet bag. Into his hand fell three large teeth and a tuft of grayish-brown fur. All of us leaned closer to see the objects, even Pudgy, who wasn't scared anymore. After Jess returned the items to the bag and tucked it into this shirt, Dad said it was time for us kids to get to bed. But we weren't ready to sleep yet, because the story Jess told us didn't explain what had happened just before he emerged from the trees. Even though he said the howling was him, we weren't convinced. Something in the tone of his laugh stuck with us, especially Carlton, who had the nerve to ask him. As if the night hadn't been strange enough, when Jess was asked about the second howling, he looked shocked. He said he always heard the howling when he came into the hills on the Moon of the Chokecherries, but he had never known anyone else who heard it. He paused to let the words sink in. 'Boys, the first howl you heard was me, but the second one, I promise, was not.' Now even Dad was puzzled.

"Finally, Jess spoke again. 'You know, that cave isn't very far from here. Maybe a few hour's walk.' Before anyone could speak, Jess knew what was racing through our minds. He turned to Dad and asked, 'What about I take you and the boys over to the cave tomorrow?' Jess paused and then added in a whisper, 'I believe you all are supposed to go there.' How could we refuse?

"After breakfast the next morning, Jess led us down the valley and into the hills. Along the way, no one said much. If Jess hadn't been with us, we never would have noticed the opening in the rocks. It was obscured by two boulders resting against each other. Inside, the cave was big enough that Jess and two of us boys could go in together at a time. Carlton and I went first. The floor was packed dirt, and the walls were black stone. Jess held the torch high to the ceiling so we could look around. On the back wall, we saw the painting of a wolf, sitting on its haunches, head in the air.

"After everyone had seen the cave and we were all outside sitting on the outcrop, Jess answered our questions about the painting. 'I put that painting there. As far as I know, this was the last wolf ever to roam the Paha Sapa. I wanted it to always have a home.' He dropped his head for a moment. Finally he said, 'We better be going. There's the walk back.' Jess guided us most of the way back to camp but left us once he was sure we were on the path to Greasy Grass. Before heading into the woods, he gathered us boys around him and said, 'Boys, like I said last night, you are the first ones who have ever heard the old wolf howl. It was not by accident. Nothing like this happens by accident. You may not understand this until you're older, but you will.'

"That night was our last before heading out to the train and home, and we boys sat around waiting for the howling to begin again. Our eager ears were disappointed. Sometime during the talk about our day with Jess, Pudgy asked the question that has forever haunted me: 'Do you think that when Jess howls the old wolf answers him?'"

Julian stood and poked at the campfire with a long branch. "And that's the story," he said quietly.

Doc expressed the doubt circling through everyone's mind. "Okay, guys, do you really expect us to believe that you heard some old ghost wolf howling to you?"

Carlton and Julian looked at each other and shrugged their shoulders. "You believe what you want," Julian began. "You can doubt us if you wish, but we know what happened." The way he said it made the others begin doubting their skepticism.

That evening, The Gentlemen's Society of Angling engaged in the age-old game of topping-the-previous-guy's-story. The phrase "okay, but one time when I was . . ." passed from man to man. It was this dimension the Osgoods brought to the group, an unending youthful enthusiasm permeating all that they did. Doc described it as impulsiveness. Bart figured it to be an all-out refusal to grow up. Inside of every man is a boy wanting to break out. Regardless, the Osgood brothers were secretly admired and envied.

Well, the secret is out! Doc had another story in Sports Afield, *only this time it's about these five guys who have this fishing cabin in the mountains. Hmm, wonder who that could be? The story tells about the time two of the guys tried to build glasses that would allow them to see underwater to watch trout. Of course, this is more than loosely connected to the events perpetrated by Julian and Bart who, one day when they were here alone, tried this very thing.*

Bart, ever the inventor, took an old can and glued a piece of glass on one of the open ends. Then, he and Julian went down to the creek and stuck it in the water to look below the surface. Surprisingly, it worked. They didn't have much luck seeing the fish, though. Every time they put it in the water, they'd see only shadows swimming away. The one thing they did see were all the insects crawling on the bottom. At one point, Bart began lifting rocks off the bottom upstream of Julian so he could watch them float down the Laurel.

Doc made all this into quite a tale. He has a real knack for making us see more than we experience. Maybe this is why he's a good doctor. Anyway, I bet all the guys who have read Doc's magazine story wish they were us. At least he didn't tell them where they could find us. Some secrets should never be revealed.

I wonder where the viewing can is?

Carlton, April 1949

Jack

Jack showed up today with a brand new pair of the rubberized Hodgeman hippers. Of course, we all had to try them on. Jack, with his usual thoroughness, explained that these had the latest advancements in materials and that even the seams up the legs were glued and sealed. We let him have the first try, but we pressured him enough that he let us each have a go—well, all of us except me. I couldn't fit in them. Jack just about blew a gasket as he watched me slide my big legs into them. The seams began to creak and moan and finally Jack yelled at me to stop before I ripped them out.

These are the first hippers to have the boots built right into the pants. You just take off your regular boots, slide your legs in, tie the side straps around your belt, and get to it.

It wasn't until we walked back up to the cabin that the rest of us fully appreciated what Jack had. We were all stripping off wet pants to change, then Jack slid off the hippers and was bone dry. I predict there will be several orders placed at Smitty's come Monday! I wonder if they make them in my size? It'll probably cost me more.

Barton, August 10, 1936

Outside, the smoke from the trains and the mills filled the air with a mixture of gray haze that rose up Mt. Washington as the sun warmed the air. Trains bringing in tons of ore rumbled through unnoticed on their way to the mills, another of Pittsburgh's contributions to the war, while passenger cars bound for New York idled next to platforms on the other side of the numerous gates leading off to each side of the main terminal. The pervasive color of attire inside Penn Station was olive drab, a soldier color. There was an overwhelming aura of pride and fear mixed with the color. Everywhere the eye turned around the Grand Hall, embraces reluctantly divided and re-engaged like rhythmic dances staged against the art deco walls and recently painted murals that had been commissioned by the WPA. Mothers and sons. Fathers and sons. Wives and husbands. Brothers and sisters. Young romances barely understood.

Jack Langsenkamp shouldered up to his son Charlie as Frances peered down into the Brownie to frame the husband and son she so dearly loved. "My, my how things change," she whispered to Janie, her daughter. She looked up at them as they posed each with an arm still wrapped around the other's shoulder. Frances could see Jack in their son. The bright, green eyes were the same ones she remembered noticing the summer Jack was working at Switz's General Store. The long, lean body of her son, topped with a head of bristly-black hair, stretched above Jack. They were both as handsome as ever. She smiled through her thoughts until a question entered. How does it work that her child had to answer for the problems of others?—the same question repeated in different forms by thousands of other parents watching sons depart for war.

A series of whistles blew one after another down the hall, calling each unit into formation. Charlie smiled at his mom and stepped forward between the arms she still wished could shield him. He gave Janie, his ten-year-old sister, a kiss on the cheek and tussled her hair. He turned to Jack, shook his hand, and said, "Gotta go." Grabbing his rifle and duffel, he headed to join the other young men, then suddenly stopped and turned back to his dad . "Hey, Dad. You tell Big Sam I'm coming back to see him again."

"Count on it," Jack said, with a little wink for emphasis.

Jack quickly grabbed Frances when he sensed her knees giving way. Her tiny shoulders trembled. Janie squeezed between them. They watched as Charlie took his position among the seemingly countless rows of uniforms forming impeccably straight lines down the length of the Grand Hall, row after row, column after column, units of fifty men each. Charlie snapped to attention with an audible "Sir!" when his name was called. The men stood in silence as the pattern repeated itself. "Slayton." "Sir!" "Stout." "Sir!" With the last name called, the sergeant turned to his left and said, "All present and accounted for, sir." The captain gestured with his head toward the trains. The sergeant saluted and turned to the troops. "Company D, leeeeeeft face." There was a swish and a snap of boot heels. "Forward, march."

Two-by-two the soldiers disappeared through the archway to the loading platforms. Now Jack and Frances were supporting each other. Both wanted to sit down, but all of the benches were occupied. "Let's go. There's nothing else for us here," Jack said. They fell in line behind the others heading for the exits. It was hard for Jack to see faces, with so many buried in the corners of shoulders or bent forward staring blankly at the marble floor stretching out before them. They prayed they weren't going to be the ones to receive the telegram, but they also knew not everyone would be spared. Jack and Frances stopped to talk with friends whose youngest son was in Charlie's outfit. The Broadhursts now had a son fighting on both fronts. Wishing each other well, the families bid their good-byes.

Jack opened the door to the Dodge for Frances, aiding her slightly as she slid into the seat. Only when they pulled onto the road did Frances's tears begin to spill down her cheeks. Janie's sobs followed from the backseat. Frances had held up well, he thought. She had always been a small woman, even when she carried Charlie and Janie. She had always worn her hair long, but now that some gray had started to creep into it, she had started rolling and pinning it in the back. Jack thought it made her look older than her forty-two years and told her so. Shortly after they turned onto the highway heading southeast out of Pittsburgh toward Ligonier, Frances broke the silence with a statement that bottomed in the pit of his stomach.

"We'll never see him again."

From the back, Janie emphatically howled, "Don't say that, Mom."

Jack didn't know how to respond. His wife had never been a pessimist, and he hoped there was nothing to the idea of women's intuition. "He's a great kid, Frances. He knows how to take care of himself. We'll make sure we throw a big party when he gets back." He knew his words would not soothe or reassure her, or himself for that matter. Silence, broken only by whimpers, returned.

Frances broke into their thoughts again. "Jack. Who is Big Sam?"

"Big Sam?"

"Yeah, who's this Big Sam guy? Is it one of Jack's friends? Janie, do you know?" she asked, throwing an arm over the seat to glance back. "I don't remember him knowing anyone named Sam," she added, tucking another withered tissue into her purse.

"Big Sam is a fish," Jack replied.

"What do you mean it's a fish?"

"Big Sam is a brook trout that lives, well, used to live, in Laurel Creek by the cabin. Charlie is the only person who ever caught Big Sam." Jack sensed pride rising in his voice.

"Is it a good story, this one about Charlie catching Big Sam?"

"Yeah, it's a great story," he said.

After a short pause, Frances turned to her husband and said, "Tell me about it, Jack. I need a good story right now. A happy story. Especially one that involves Charlie."

Jack took a deep breath and began. "It was six years ago when I took Charlie up to the cabin for his birthday. You remember the argument we had when I called school to tell them Charlie was sick?"

"Oh, do I ever. I believe I said something about you were teaching the boy bad habits." She chuckled softly.

"I believe the words were more in the realm of mortal sin than bad habits, but you certainly made your point," he returned through a sly grin. "Well, we'd spent most of that Friday fishing different spots where I knew Charlie could wade without my having to worry about him falling in or hurting himself. God, that was a beautiful fall day. I don't think I've ever seen a day more beautiful. The trees were in full color but hadn't yet begun to drop their leaves. The bushes overhanging the banks were brilliant yellow, and their reflections in the blue water made them look like gold pieces tossed in the creek to adorn it. Charlie had a great day fishing. I couldn't begin to tell you how many fish he caught, though I bet to this day he could." Frances nodded in agreement. "I remember how hard it was to get him to stop long enough to have some lunch. You know Charlie—when he gets going at something, he doesn't stop until he's near exhaustion."

"Yeah, like when he makes me help do chores," Janie interjected.

Jack glanced at his wife to see her gazing out the window into the trees. "Later that afternoon I realized we were a long way downstream from the cabin and told Charlie it was time we head back. Of course, he didn't want to go. But he finally gave in when I reminded him it was only Friday and we had two more days ahead of us. On the way back to the cabin, we walked by this rock wall along the creek where there's a deep spot. Shortly after Charlie walked over to the edge and looked down into the water, this big shadow shot across the water and then back under the ledge he was standing on. He screamed 'Dad' so loud I first thought he had fallen in. By the time I got to him, he was panting and pointing down into the water. He kept saying, 'Was that a fish I saw down there?'

"While Charlie lay down to try to see farther under the overhang, I grabbed his ankles so he wouldn't roll over the edge. I explained to him that the shadow was of Big Sam, and that he was the granddaddy of all the fish in the creek. He immediately wanted to know if he could drop a bug into the water to see if he could catch him. As much as I wanted to let him, I told him that maybe we could give it a try tomorrow. Big Sam was all he could talk about on the rest of the walk back to the cabin.

"When we got there, Doc and Julian were just sitting down to a big pot of stew. We joined them, and of course the first question out of Charlie's mouth was about Big Sam. I think it was Doc who took up the story and spun out the tale of Big Sam. He told Charlie that for years anglers had tried everything they could think of to try to catch Big Sam, but that old fish was too smart to fall prey to a bunch of feathers."

Frances interrupted. "So what Charlie meant at the station was that he didn't want anyone to catch Big Sam before he gets back."

"Well, not exactly. Well, maybe. See, Doc and Julian continued to embellish stories about Big Sam, and Charlie soaked it all in. Julian kept saying that only a first-class fisherman could coax Big Sam to a fly. You know how he loves teasing Charlie. What none of us realized was that Charlie was hatching a plan to catch Big Sam. I guess I should have suspected something was up when Charlie began tying flies the likes of which I had never seen. I mean to tell you, those things didn't resemble anything Mother Nature created. There was no way a wary trout would come calling to one of them, though one that looked somewhat like a praying mantis eventually surprised us. If I hadn't finally laid down the law, I think Charlie would have sat there all night tying flies.

"The next morning, we were sitting around with a cup of coffee when we heard Charlie screaming down by the creek.

We were shocked because we thought he was still in his bunk. He had bunched up his blankets to make it look as if he was still under them."

"Hmm, I remember how he did that one day at home and almost was late for school." Frances giggled.

"Anyway, we all raced down to the water trying to locate Charlie, and the whole time he was yelling at the top of his lungs. Finally, we headed downstream and saw him kneeling in the middle of the stream. As we rushed into the water, we could finally hear that Charlie was screaming. 'I caught Big Sam! I caught Big Sam!'"

Frances looked at her husband but said nothing about the tear edging its way down his cheek. "So what did you do? Was Charlie okay?"

After a pause, Jack continued. "I'm sure anyone else seeing us would have thought it was a pretty strange sight—three grown men standing in the water over a boy with his hand holding a trout down on the pebbles. I don't think anyone said a word. We were just too stunned to speak, probably. I think it was Charlie who broke the silence. If I remember right, he said, 'Is this Big Sam?' Eventually, we were all kneeling down looking at the most beautiful fish any of us had ever seen. The red-orange fins with white edges on Big Sam made the leaves on the trees fade in shame. And sticking out of the corner of that fish's mouth was the big gaudy praying mantis fly. You know what Charlie did then? He looked at me and asked if he could let the fish go.

"I'll tell you, Frances, I didn't know whether to laugh or cry. Here we had all spent years trying to catch this damn fish, Charlie gets the job done, and he wants to let it go."

"What did you tell him?" Frances asked.

"I told him it was totally up to him."

"And?"

"He picked up that fish like it was a newborn baby and set it out farther in the stream. He was kneeling in the water just watching, running his hands down it like it was a hurt puppy. A few minutes later, Big Sam gave a little swish of his tail and headed off back home. I don't think I've ever been prouder of Charlie than I was at that moment."

Jack suddenly noticed that Frances had reached across the seat and was holding his hand. When she squeezed it gently, he looked at her. His expression spoke his thoughts. They again rode on for a while without speaking. Janie was asleep across the backseat.

"Has anyone caught Big Sam since then?" Frances asked.

"Oh, I'm sure Big Sam is long gone. That was several years ago, and trout don't live that long," he responded.

"Then why did Charlie say he'd be back to see Big Sam?" she asked sincerely.

"I don't know. Maybe it was his way of saying he'll be okay."

Frances detected a hint of doubt in his voice but didn't say anything. They were nearly home. She next spoke when the car had come to a stop in the driveway. "Jack, why don't you go up to the cabin for the rest of the day? I have some things to do around here, and you'll just be in the way." He didn't respond. Frances woke Janie and helped her out of the car. Jack put an arm around his wife's waist and walked her toward the house.

A half hour later, Jack appeared in the kitchen dressed in a pair of work pants and shirt. He kissed his wife on the cheek and said, "I'll be out in the garage. Maybe I'll go up to the cabin tomorrow." She kissed him back and gave him a smile that reminded him of the one he had fallen in love with many years earlier. She watched him move down the sidewalk, stop to pull a weed from a crack, then toss it into the honeysuckle bushes. In one way she felt lucky. Jack had not been called into service. Jeannie Kopeck's husband Bill was Jack's age and he had been drafted. She thought how strange that Jack's irregular heartbeat, something that could one day kill him, kept him from a likely death at the hands of others. Jack had put on weight. It was the first time she noticed that his middle was as wide as his shoulders. Despite this, his coal-black hair helped him retain a youthful look. He slipped through the side door of the garage. She returned to slicing apples.

It was almost evening when she called to him that dinner was ready. There was no response. After her second call got no response, she walked out to the garage and found Jack sitting in the corner with a fishing rod draped across his lap. She stood in front of him to get his attention.

"Jack, you okay?" she asked quietly.

"This is the rod Bart gave Charlie. It's the one he learned to fish with," Jack whispered.

"Is that the one he caught Big Sam with?"

Jack looked up and smiled. "Yep."

"Well, when you're finished, supper's on the table," she said, returning his smile. "I made an apple pie," she added with artificial cheerfulness in her voice.

"I'll be right in."

Just as she closed the door she detected the faint sound of

his breath being exhaled in a sigh. She wanted to turn around but knew better. It was as much for his sake as her own.

Jack thought back to the day Bart had given Charlie the rod. He remembered how Charlie peppered him with questions as they drove into town to pick out a reel and line—Charlie's impatience as they wound the line on the reel and slipped it into the seat, Charlie running to the creek, his son's first few casts with the line piled up in the water or tangled in the overhanging limbs, the bag of flies the guys put together in their absence. It didn't matter that Charlie didn't catch a fish that day. Jack remembered it as a perfect day to be a father.

The next day, Jack left early for the cabin. Frances heard the Dodge pull out about five o'clock. On the drive out of town, Jack began rolling thoughts through his head about what Charlie was doing. He posed questions to himself and attempted answers. Had they arrived in New York yet? *Let's see, a train leaving Pittsburgh and then stopping at Philadelphia could travel to New York in less than twenty-four hours. So yes, Charlie was there.* Wonder if they'll stay in New York more than a day or go straight to the ships? *There must be thousands of men, boys, waiting to organize into larger units. That had to take a day or more. So no, Charlie wasn't at sea yet.*

The thoughts rolled on and on as he drove farther into the mountains. It was in these mountains, these woods, where he had watched Charlie grow up. More had happened here than merely Big Sam. Their life together filtered through the trees to mix with the water. Here's where Charlie tasted his first beer. Here's where Charlie learned to tie flies. Here's where Charlie. . . . He pushed the thoughts away as he eased his car into the pull-off next to Julian's truck.

He grabbed his satchel and the rod case lying across the backseat and began the descent down the path. Walking deeper into the trees, he could feel the air cool as the shade enveloped him. He could hear voices and smell the smoke from the outside fire. As he walked around the corner of the cabin, the voices suddenly stopped. Julian and Barton rose and turned toward him. It was Jack who spoke first. "You guys come down last night or this morning?"

Barton ignored the question. "Charlie get off okay?"

Jack successfully reined in his emotions. "Yeah. His train left yesterday morning about eight."

"Here, let me help you with that stuff," Julian said, rushing over and grabbing the satchel and rod case. Jack's grip on the rod case was too strong, and Julian's hand slid down the length of the leather tube. Barton recognized the rod case as Charlie's.

"Thanks, but I can manage." There was a tone of resentment in his voice that was gone in seconds. "Let's put this inside and I'll tell you about it."

Later, Jack told them about the events in Pittsburgh while the three men leaned against the logs that encircled the fire pit. Julian and Bart listened intently as Jack described the scene of row after row of boys and men heading out through the tunnels to the trains. He named the ones he knew. Phil Lawrence's boy, Phil Junior. Harry Broadhurst. Peter Stevens. Some of these boys had been in his history class at Highland High. Jack recounted how the school had changed once the war in the Pacific started. Almost overnight, military personnel appeared at schoolhouse doors across the country to alter physical education classes. The strength of America now rested on training for war. Even his own history class changed. Now he helped organize scrap drives. The focus wasn't on understanding American history but on making sure there was a country that could have a history. When he had nothing more to tell, they sat in silence.

Finally, Julian asked gently, "Jack, we were just about to grab our rods when you showed up. What say we all head down to the creek and see if the fish are biting?"

Jack knew the intent of the invitation was more for him than anyone. Immediately he wondered why he was here. Without pause he said, "Why don't you two go ahead, and I'll come down in a few minutes. There are some things I want to do first."

Julian looked at Barton and gestured with his head toward the creek. As they stood up, Julian turned to Jack. "We're going to head upstream. Join us when you're done, okay?"

Jack smiled and rose. "I'll be there in a little bit." He watched them head down the path as he turned toward the cabin. Inside, he glanced down at Charlie's rod case lying on the table. He removed the leather cap from the end and let the cloth bag slide out into his hands. Piece by piece, he assembled the rod and slipped the reel into the seat, again thinking of the day Bart had given the rod to Charlie. He walked to the rod rack on the wall, opened the leather strap, slipped the rod into the half circle cut in the upper railing, and slid the strap back onto the nailhead that held it across the opening. He set the butt and reel behind the strip of wood that formed the lip along the bottom rail. Stepping back for a moment, he studied the pair of rods nestled next to each other. So much joy had been achieved with these two rods. They were as much family as the two who owned them. He closed his eyes for a moment. Eventually, he undid the strap across his own Horrocks-Ibbotson and pulled it from the rack. Jack thought, I should just go to the water. There's nothing I can do to change what's happened.

He backed out the door, making sure that it didn't slam and break his rod. Nearly at the end of the path, he stopped along the water's edge, turning quickly to a voice from behind. "Charlie?" As soon as the name was out of his mouth, he felt foolish. He let out a quiet chuckle that was more air than sound. He started to head downstream toward the spot where Charlie had caught Big Sam but then thought better of it. Turning to his right, he headed upstream toward the faint voices bouncing through the trees.

The rest of the day, Jack was able to get his mind off Charlie periodically. The cool water around his legs and the earthy pine aroma aided the escape. The fish helped too. That evening the three men sat around the campfire talking about the war and of course Charlie. Jack brought it up. It was his way of letting his two friends know that they need not be cautious with their words.

Later in the evening, Barton went into the cabin and returned with three glasses of whiskey. He handed one to Julian and one to Jack. "Jack, I'd like to propose a toast to Charlie." Julian and Jack stood. "To Charlie. Godspeed." Glasses clicked. Each man drank fully.

The next morning as Jack started outdoors to get the fire going to boil up a pot of coffee, he noticed something had been added to the wall behind the rack of rods. The sun was barely up and the cabin still dark, so he opened the door to brighten up things a little. He moved to the wall and realized the addition was a photograph. Peering closer, he saw it was the picture his friends had taken of him and Charlie standing together in the creek the morning Big Sam had been landed. They were silhouetted by the morning sun at their backs as it reflected through the mist lifting off the water. Jack wasn't sure whether to laugh or cry. He did both. He lingered for a moment, then went out to make the coffee. Sitting alone with his favorite blue graniteware cup steaming between his hands, he thought about Charlie and wondered if he, too, was sitting with the day's first cup.

Godspeed, son.

> *The Westmoreland County Commissioners are propos- ing that the road we use to get up here be widened and paved to make it easier for folks to get from Greensburg to Johnstown. I suppose this comes with change, the inevitable encroachment of modern life into everything we do.*
>
> *I guess what this means is that our promise to focus only on fishing, as we said in our creed, is being pushed to the side. Maybe we're just getting too old. Now we're old geezers sitting around the cabin wishing we were young again. But I feel sorry for the young people now. They don't bring their kids to fish; they have them help build backyard fallout shelters. They take them out to watch satellites pass across the evening sky, threatening them from above. They look to heaven not to wonder about its vastness and purpose but to analyze it as a new frontier to conquer and control. Somehow, I think we in The Society felt there was a heaven here on earth to explore. That all seems so terribly lost now.*
>
> *Jack, 1961*

Barton

There are times when the gestures of others add to our lives in ways that are beyond understanding. Hands of friendship reach out and direct us toward a larger understanding of what constructs life and humaneness. There is no finer example than when a friend acts in such a way that members of another family more clearly understand the richness of their lives together.

It seems unreal how a simple refuge from the world, like this cabin, brings out the finest in people. Maybe it's not that what we have here causes us to change. Rather, it's that we have the opportunity to trust and be trusted to act in ways that honor the human spirit. Just as we attempt to reach out to the natural world with our rods and flies to become, momentarily, part of it, so do the acts of others reach out and catch hold of what is inside each of us. We become more than ourselves here. Bart has proved that beyond doubt.

Jack, August 1938

"Doc," Julian began, "this is Barton Schoeppner."

"Just Bart, please."

"Bart, it's a pleasure. Julian and Carlton have told me lots of good things about you," Doc said extending a hand. Doc was surprised by the man's size. Despite the Osgoods' descriptions comparing him to a tree trunk, Doc found Bart much more imposing than that. He couldn't imagine sitting across a desk from Bart to work out a loan. Even more unlikely was seeing the towering man holding a fishing rod. In his hands it looked like a cherry tree switch intended for a young rascal's bottom.

"What say we get to the water," Bart interjected.

"You two go ahead. I need to get my rod inside. Where you taking Bart, Julian?"

"I thought we'd just head straight in and fish the rock field," Julian answered.

"Great. I'll be right down," Doc said, finishing his sentence on the way to the cabin. By the time he joined them, Julian had Bart placed in the spot Doc imagined, just upstream from the exposed rocks but far enough into the current to minimize line drag. Obviously it had worked, as Bart's rod was bending against the weight of the fish heading downstream.

After his fish was dropped into the creel, Bart saw Doc easing into the water. "Hell of a place you've got here." With that, he turned again toward the rocks and began casting.

Doc stopped to watch. Despite Bart's size, close to 300 pounds, the man handled the rod fairly well. He tended to overpower the rod, but his accuracy was excellent. On each cast, the fly hit the water several feet upstream of a rock and gently drifted down the feeding lane. Doc noticed that Bart was fishing a wet fly. He didn't know whether this was Bart's choice or because no bugs were floating on the surface film. Either way, it worked, because Doc heard him say, "There's another one." Julian waved from upstream, so Doc headed the other way.

At midday the three of them were leaning back in their chairs in front of the fireplace. The weather, even for early October, had taken a marked turn toward winter. The morning had given way to an ashen sky, a reminder that when it wanted to snow, it would. Their wet boots and rubberized muslin pants steamed as they dried next to the fire, filling the cabin with a mist that was swirled by the draft edging under the door.

"You know, guys," Bart began, "this day reminds me of working the hay fields when I was a kid. Damn, that was miserable work. Doc, you ever cut hay?" The head shake no gave him the okay to continue. "Damn miserable work. We'd head out about sunup wrapped up in coats and stuff, and by noon we were either freezing or so damn hot we were bare-chested. I can remember days like this one where it'd be beautiful and all of a sudden it would snow. It's bad enough getting dry hay down inside your clothes, but the wet stuff was the worst. It would just rub your back raw." He paused for a moment and again exclaimed, "Damn miserable work."

They spent the rest of the afternoon listening to Bart tell stories about growing up in Mt. Lebanon and working on the farm. Finally, Doc asked, "So, Bart, how does a farm kid end up a banker in Pittsburgh?"

"By the time I got to high school, I saw all the town kids having fun while I was stuck doing chores. Then and there I promised myself to find an easier way to get through life. So when I got the chance to play ball at Pitt, I made sure I didn't blow the opportunity. Of course, with what's been going on these past few years, I don't know whether haying or banking is worse."

Although all The Society's members had suffered some from the economic plunge, the time they spent at the cabin pushed the hard times away. Here, for them, the river and the fish and the woods filled the well of hope that had gone dry for so many others. At the cabin, they thought about things other than business and money, the poor conditions across the country, the drought in the West. They knew the future was uncertain. Still, wasn't it adversity that spurred people on to accomplish more in life?

For Bart, the challenges he faced had eased after the banking industry's government-forced holidays had stabilized the system. He began thinking about other opportunities. Although he could afford to buy most things he needed, the creative process of working with tools ingrained in him as a farm boy always pushed him forward. After meeting Charlie, Jack's son, at the cabin and watching his frustration at having to fish with a makeshift stick, Bart thought of building a fly rod. Of course, the problem was he had no idea how to begin.

Through a series of correspondence, he was surprised to learn that his own Montague rod had been built at Farlow's in Philadelphia. He also discovered that workers at Farlow's had been trained by a man who lived in Kittanning. He decided to try to arrange a visit.

Frank Pharis, who had been building rods for almost sixty years, was at one time the primary constructor and had apprenticed many others in the fine art of planing and gluing bamboo strips. He was just the person Bart wanted to meet. He had sent Pharis a letter, but no reply had come back.

Although Bart hesitated to drop by unannounced, he didn't see that he had a choice if he was serious about learning the ropes. As he drove the sixty miles to Kittanning, he began fabricating his explanation. "Let's see . . ."

Eventually, he spotted the correct mailbox number and eased the car into the driveway. He still wasn't sure what to say, or even do, for that matter. Bart noticed that the yard and sidewalk were in disrepair. The wooden steps leading up to the porch creaked under his weight. A few moments after knocking on the door, a man opened it a crack. "Excuse me, sir, I'm Bart Schoeppner. Are you Frank Pharis?"

"What're you selling?" Pharis asked abruptly as he closed the door slightly. "If you're looking for a handout, I can't help you."

"No, Mr. Pharis, I'm not selling anything or looking for a handout. I sent you a letter about building fly rods. Do you recall receiving it?"

"Of course I remember it. You think I'm too old to remember?" Pharis had a definite edge to his voice. This was going much worse than Bart had hoped.

"Mr. Pharis, I didn't mean that at all. You see, when I didn't hear from you, I just—." Bart didn't get to finish.

"Fine, fine. So, what can I do for you?"

"You used to build fly rods, didn't you?" Pharis nodded his head slightly. "I wondered if you could help me learn how to build one." Bart noticed that Pharis's attitude had tempered some, as he no longer had his arms folded across his chest.

"Why do you want to build a fishing pole? Buying one's a whole lot easier."

Bart wasn't sure he knew himself. "I thought it would be a good idea to have more than one rod." As soon as he said it, he knew that wasn't the reason.

Pharis's tone was sarcastic. "Why? You can't fish with two rods at the same time, can you?"

Bart felt like a schoolboy being grilled by the principal. "Look, I've always liked building things since I was a farm kid. Nowadays, I don't do that. I also like fishing." The more he babbled on, the more his mind cluttered with thoughts. Why was he here?

Pharis stood looking at him, letting him ramble through his lame explanations. When Bart finally exhausted his words, Pharis said, "Follow me." Bart followed him down the four steps and around the side of the white clapboard house. They were heading toward a shed near the back corner of the yard. Bart noticed that three sides of the shed were glass. Outside the shed were several barrels overflowing with sawdust. Pharis opened the door and latched it open with a hook against the side. Bart followed Pharis's instructions and ducked under the door header that was little more than six feet off the ground.

Inside, the light filtering in through the glass walls cast a gentle glow across a long workbench with numerous vises screwed into its edges. The one solid wall held a full array of tools neatly organized on shelves. Hand planes dominated most of the space. A quick glance told Bart there must be at least twenty. In one corner, two barrels were filled with various lengths and sizes of bamboo sticks. On the west wall, several wooden pegs spaced about eight inches apart formed columns jutting out from the window casings. Pieces of bamboo lay horizontally across the pegs. Bart wandered around the workbench sitting in the middle of the room. A metal jig about five feet long was held in place by two of the vises along the bench. Down the length of it was a small V-groove. He walked over to the tools. The hand planes, some no bigger than a fat mouse, lay on their sides along the shelves. He wanted to pick them up for a look but felt it would be inappropriate. He stuffed his hands in his pockets and turned to Pharis. "I don't think I've ever seen so many planes in my life. Do you use all of these?"

The rod builder was leaning against the workbench. "Why are you here, Schoeppner?"

Bart was stunned by the bluntness of the question. As he formulated an answer, he studied Pharis's features. He figured Pharis must be at least seventy and couldn't have more than 150 pounds spread across his frame. The gray tufts of hair along the sides and back of his head hung like steel wool underneath his hat. "I'm not really sure, to be honest. Maybe it's because I've spent hours sitting at home looking down the seams of my Montague and been fascinated by how precisely the pieces fit together. I've been over that rod countless times, and I can't find one spot where there's a gap or even a slight imperfection in the fit. I know bamboo doesn't grow that way, but I can't for the life of me imagine how round sticks are shaped into hexagons with flat sides. But I'm beginning to get the picture." He gestured toward the planes and then looked at the jig in the vise. "Mr. Pharis," he began, walking toward him, "I want to learn how to do this. I can't really explain to you why. I just know I do. Can you help me?"

Pharis folded his arms across his chest again. "Can I help you? Of course I can. The question you want answered is, will

I teach you?" He fell silent. Although Bart towered over Pharis, Bart felt the smaller of the two men. "Before I give you an answer, let me show you how it's done and then we'll decide." With that, Pharis slipped on the apron he had grabbed off the nail next to the door. He instructed Bart to join him on the other side where the jig was anchored in the vises. "Bart, you wondered how the bamboo is shaped. Well, this is how. Pieces of raw bamboo are split off a culm—a stalk—and tested to see if they have the same tensile strength and flexibility. They're hand-shaped and laid into these jigs and then hand-planed into strips. Once the planing is done on six identical pieces, they're glued together to form a section of a rod. This process is continued by repeatedly adjusting the sides of the forms," Pharis pointed toward other jigs sitting on a shelf, "until you have all the sections made. Then you have to match the flexibility of each section so the rod will work as one unit. Of course, this is just the first step. Once the overall rod is shaped, the pieces have to be gently sanded and several coats of varnish applied. The final steps are to attach ferrules, a reel seat, and handle and to wrap the guides. Now, everything I just told you takes weeks to complete. This is not something that one does in a couple of days."

Bart was hanging intently on every word. He followed along behind Pharis wondering if this was his lesson in rod building. He felt uncomfortable asking a question that would interrupt him, but he also wanted to get his hands on the equipment.

Finally, Pharis stopped talking and fixed his gaze on Bart. "Mr. Schoeppner, you asked if I could help you learn how to do all this. Well, no I can't." Bart's stomach hit bottom. "I can teach you what to do, but if you want to learn it, that's up to you," Pharis said firmly. Bart knew what he meant. Commitment was the student's responsibility to assume or reject. It was clear that an answer was expected right then and there. Bart could tell that Pharis was not one to waste time. Maybe that comes with age. Pharis saw Bart's hesitancy and began to move toward the door.

"Mr. Pharis, I want to learn how to do this. If it means coming here to learn from you, then you can count on me to be here. Look, I'm pretty handy with tools, and if I learned anything on the farm, it was that the best things that happen in life come from hard work. If you're wondering whether I'll be able to learn all this, I can't answer you. But I can assure you that if you'll give me the chance, and your time, I'll put my best effort into it. You tell me what you want me to do, and I'll do it."

Pharis moved closer to him. "Son, I've taught some of the best rod makers in this country and one or two in England. The only thing I ever asked of them was that they work hard at learning the craft. If you're willing to give me that type of promise, I'll show you how to build a rod."

Bart looked at him and said, "When do we start?"

The first smile Bart had seen from the man edged across his stubbled chin. It seemed to dip back into the sides of his face and make his cheeks glow pink. "I'll tell you what, it's too late to start anything this afternoon. You stop by tomorrow morning early and we'll get started. How does that sound?"

"Can you tell me where I can get a room around these parts?" Bart said, matching the smile. They walked out into the side yard of the house. The brightness of the sun hurt

Bart's eyes. They parted ways with Bart heading into town to locate the Franklin Rooming House.

That evening, Bart sat wishing he could stretch his rod across his lap and examine the sections. Since seeing Pharis's planing forms, his amazement had grown. The pieces must fit together so precisely, he couldn't imagine the amount of work that went into the task.

Bart wasn't sure what to expect as the first light of morning sun rolled over the trees of the hills along the road back to Pharis's house. His stomach rumbled the way it did the day he rode the bus to school the first day. There was one difference, though—this time he knew what the teacher was like. But he couldn't decide whether Pharis would act as he had the day before or be totally different. Bart thought he had good reason to believe that his first lesson would be intense.

Pulling into the driveway, he noticed how the lights glowing inside the shed silhouetted Pharis bent over the workbench. As Bart entered the open door of the shed, Pharis looked up at him and smiled. "There's a cup and some coffee over in the corner if you want some." He immediately turned back to planing the strip of wood clamped into the jig. Bart poured himself a cup but wasn't sure what to do next. Pharis gave him the answer. "Do me a favor and turn out the lights. There's enough sunlight now that we can work without them." Bart set his cup down and began walking around the perimeter walls pulling the bead chains dangling under each light. He wondered what time Pharis had started working. His watch read 6:30 A.M. "Bart, come over here and have a look at this piece and tell me if you think it's level with the form."

Stepping into the space Pharis had vacated, Bart looked down at the piece. "Can I run my finger down it?"

"Sure, that's fine."

Bart slid his index finger down the length of the bamboo wedged into the groove. He couldn't feel any imperfections or bumps but wasn't sure. Here was his first challenge. "The wood feels level with the sides, but wouldn't it be more precise to use a level or something rather than a finger? What are the tolerances supposed to be at different points down the piece?"

When Bart looked up at Pharis, he noticed the smile. "Son, you just passed your first test." He reached into his apron pocket and pulled out a caliper and handed it to Bart. Reaching down, he undid the clamps at the side of the jig and pulled out the strip of wood. "The taper should be two-thirds from this line," Pharis pointed to the marks on the piece, "to this line. Measure the base and then the tip and tell me what you get." Bart spread the caliper tines apart and gently squeezed them until they touched both edges of the stick. He wrote the numbers on a piece of paper Pharis had laid on the bench. After measuring at the other mark, he did the division and handed Pharis the piece of paper. Pharis handed it back to him. "So, how did I do?"

Bart's anxiety rose as he studied the paper. "If my arithmetic's right, the taper isn't quite right. But I have a question. How do you know which end to shave down more? I mean, you could plane or sand either end and make the math work, but that doesn't really answer whether you have the right shape. Don't you need a baseline mark to begin with?"

Before he could continue, Pharis spoke. "Bart, you just passed test number two. You really have worked with tools before, haven't you?" He paused and walked over to the coffeepot in the corner for a refill. He motioned for Bart to join him as he slid up two stools to the other side of the bench. Before sitting down, he blew dust off a small brown leather book he retrieved from the shelf behind him. As Pharis slid onto the stool, he asked, "Okay, how long do you want this rod to be? Eight feet? Twelve feet?" Bart shrugged for lack of an answer. "What weight line do you want? HD? HC?" Bart again didn't know the answer. Pharis chuckled. "Let's go about this a different way. What sort of fishing do you do?"

"Most of the time I fish over in Laurel Creek. Some friends and I have a cabin over there that we bought a few years ago. Do you know the Laurel?"

"No, I can't say that I do," Pharis answered. "Is it trout or bass or what that you fish for?"

"Oh, brook trout are the targets of our affection. The Laurel is such a great little stream. There are other types of fish in the creek, naturally, but we're there for the trout."

"I see." Pharis paused long enough to grab the brown book off the table. As he thumbed across the pages, he began an explanation. "Bart, this book contains all the specifications for the different pieces for different types of rods. Let me show you. Let's take you, for example." Bart nodded. "For someone your size, I'd recommend an eight- or eight-and-a-half-foot rod and no more than a size D. Maybe a C, but a D will allow you to use it without overpowering the rod. Also, you're pretty tall, so I'd suggest you make a two- rather than a three-piece rod, although the difference is fairly insignificant. The main difference between a two- and three-section rod is flexibility." Pharis laid the book open to a page that across the top read 8-2-D (HD). The main body of the page was a chart. To read it, the book had to be turned on its side. The left-hand edge of the chart was divided into two sections labeled Tip and Base. Across the top were columns of words and numbers. The first column was labeled B-end. The next column read 1.5, the next 3, the next 4.5, and so on to the last column, which read T-end. "These numbers at the top indicate that these are the one-and-a-half-inch measuring points along each section of an eight-foot, two-piece rod. You can see that this side shows you the two sections of a rod. The numbers in the boxes under each measuring point are the caliper readings at that point. If you did a little math, you'd see that the last measurement is exactly two-thirds of the first column." Bart realized that B-end and T-end meant Base and Tip.

Pharis laid the book out in front of Bart for a closer look. "You asked about whether that piece over there needs to be shaped at the base or tip. Well, these measurements show you. That section I was just working on is just like the one you should probably build for yourself. So if you take a look at the numbers in the book and compare them with the measurements you made, which end needs work?"

Bart reached across the bench for the piece of paper. After comparing the numbers with those on the chart, he said, "The base end is too big."

"Yep. That base end needs some shaping work. However, if we're really going to know if the piece is right, we'd need to measure down the full length of the stick." Bart glanced at the piece of bamboo cradled in the V of the jig. "You see, Bart, this isn't hard work, but it's careful work. For a rod to work properly, when all six pieces are glued together, they must fit so snugly that they work as one piece of wood. Mother Nature made a great thing when she invented bamboo, and our job is to make it better for our purposes." Pharis rose and went to one end of the racks where glued sections were drying. He walked back to Bart and handed him the section. "Look at the end of this. See how each of the V-shaped pieces fit together? If it weren't for the glue lines, you couldn't even tell that there were separate sections." Bart looked at the piece closely. It was the first time he had ever seen a fly rod section from this perspective. "How about a fresh cup of coffee and then we'll get to work? When you're done with that, just lay it over on that third level of drying racks." Pharis grabbed both cups.

While Bart looked over the pages in the book, Pharis placed the cup of coffee next to him and went to the barrel containing whole and split pieces of raw bamboo. He began looking through them one by one, occasionally pulling out a piece and setting it on the bench behind him. "Bart, when you're done over there, come here and I'll show you what to look for when you're picking out sections to cut and plane." Bart scanned a few more pages and joined Pharis at the barrel. "One of the key things you always look for when picking out a section to cut is the length of wood between the rings. Naturally, when you're looking to build a two-piece rod, you have to find somewhere close to four-and-a-half to five feet of clean stock." He turned to the sticks on the table and handed one to Bart. "Here's one that would work for the butt section of the rod you want to build. Look closely up and down the sections and you'll see that there are imperfections in the wood. You'll rarely find a piece that is perfectly clean. All you can do is find the best available. You also have to remember that all three sides of each strip gets planed, so the surface is really unimportant. It's what's underneath that counts."

Bart continued looking up and down the section as Pharis pointed out areas where the grain wasn't as tight. He explained that the main causes of the variations were the amounts of water and sunlight the bamboo received while growing. "What do you say I show you how to get started splitting the stock to get it ready for shaping?" Pharis pulled a large knife from the shelf and walked to the bench brushing the pad of his thumb across the knife edge to check its sharpness. Satisfied, he clamped the handle into one of the bench vises with the blade facing toward him. "There have been lots of methods tried, but I think this is the best. Splitting the culm is really very easy. First estimate the width of the piece and start the knife through the wood. The long, thin grains of bamboo will split easily, but you don't want to hurry this. You're trying to get whole pieces, and it's possible to have the split snap or crack, which wastes material. The best way is to gently squeeze the pieces on the backside of the knife as you draw it through.

Bart watched as Pharis began the process. He was surprised at how easily the strip separated. Pharis handed him the larger section so he could give it a shot. "We're going to start with the butt section, so make sure you cut wide enough." Bart placed the end of the culm against the knife's edge and began pushing it into the blade. "You're doing fine, but I recommend you pull more than push the stick. That will help keep the strip intact." A minute or so later, the job was done. Bart looked at the stick and compared it with the one his teacher had cut. They looked almost identical. "Okay, you see what's needed. You go ahead and split four more. While you're doing that, I'll get the jig ready."

Bart continued cutting strips while Pharis moved the planing jig he had been using to the far side of the bench. He went to the tool shelves and pulled down another one. By this time, Bart had three more strips cut and was starting the fourth. "Looks great," Pharis said, as he held up one of the strips. "The next step is to show you how to set the groove in the planing form. Remember, we're trying to shape a partial oval into a sixty-degree triangle. If you look down the sides of the form, you'll see these adjusting screws. These bring the sides of the jig closer together. The groove down the middle is exactly sixty degrees. To get started, you measure the distance between the inside edge of the V with the calipers. You adjust the distance using the side screws." Bart stepped closer to watch Pharis make the measurement. He noticed that Pharis didn't refer to the book they had been looking at. He wondered if he'd ever get that good. After setting the butt end, Pharis reached over, grabbed the book, and handed it to Bart. "You set the smaller end."

Bart turned to the page Pharis had initially shown him and set the calipers according to the number in the book. "When you set the form for the first planing, set the calipers to the exact size, then back it off one full turn. That lets you shape the strip but gives you a little to play with once you're ready for the finish cutting." Bart did as he was instructed. "Looks good, son. You're ready to begin." Bart laid one of the strips into the V, and Pharis showed him how to secure it. He went to the tool shelves and picked up the small hand plane

Pharis pointed out. "With the first few cuts, you really don't have to be overly cautious. The critical part is to make sure the plane is sharp and to keep the bottom plate flat on the form."

Bart set the plane on the two steel bars and began shaving the bamboo. He was amazed how easily the blade pared the strip. After about four passes, Pharis added further instructions. "Now you need to rotate the strip and do another side." Bart unclamped and rotated the wood. He was surprised at how tightly the side he had just planed fit against the wall of the V. After a few passes, he rotated the strip once more and planed the third side. "Now you have one of the rough strips that will form the bottom half of the rod." Pharis smiled at him. "Why don't you do the other five pieces, then we'll adjust the form for the second pass." He paused for a moment and added, "You hungry?"

The pit of Bart's stomach had the answer. Bart glanced at his watch. 11:35 A.M. They had been working nonstop for almost five hours. "Yeah, now that you mention it, I could eat something."

"You finish those, and I'll go see what's in the house. Come on up when you're done. You can see the back door just behind those bushes. There's a pump just outside the back door where you can wash up if you want."

Bart glanced toward the house and could just make out the top of the door frame. He nodded his understanding. As he watched Pharis head across the yard, it dawned on him how much he had already learned and how his fears had disappeared. Shifting his attention back to the strips in front of him, he plunged into the work. Minutes later, he took all six pieces and put them together. Although they were not completely finished, they already formed a tight hexagon. Things were starting to take shape.

As he entered the house, Pharis was standing at a counter slicing bread. He looked up as Bart entered the door. "Did they fit together?" Bart laughed aloud. He felt like a kid caught with his hand in the cookie jar. "You like ham? I've got some ham and boiled potatoes. That sound all right?"

"Yeah, that sounds great. I can't believe it's midday already."

As he put lunch on the round table set in the middle of the floor, Pharis said, "I've spent days in that shed when the sun rose and set before I ever stepped out the door." He set a plate in front of Bart. "There's just something about getting the tools in your hands and seeing the wood take shape." He slid back a chair across from Bart.

"How long have you been at this, Mr. Pharis?" Bart asked.

"First off, you can call me Frank or Pharis, but please drop the Mister." Bart acknowledged the request. "I built my first rod when I was fifteen." Bart was calculating his age, but Pharis didn't say anything. "I've been at it ever since."

"How many rods have you made?"

"Don't have any idea. Don't really care. I've never been a person who's measured his accomplishments by keeping track of his life. Always seemed to me that folks who do that eventually get to a point where they think everything is behind them. Might as well be dead as far as I'm concerned. The only thing that's of any importance is the work I'm currently doing. What about you, Bart? What do you do for a living?"

Bart was almost embarrassed to say. "I'm a banker."

"Oh, one of those." Bart was taken off guard by the response. Pharis started to laugh. "Remember a few years back when all those folks were panicking and jumping out of windows? I just couldn't understand that. You ever think about doing that?"

"No, it never crossed my mind," Bart said resolutely.

"Good. Even just knowing you a day, I can't imagine you doing something crazy like that." Pharis took a bite of bread and ham. "You got family?"

"Yeah, my wife Pat and our two daughters."

"How old are the girls?"

"Elizabeth's ten, and Katherine's six. Fortunately, they take after their mom." Pharis laughed. "How about you? Do you have family?"

"My Cindy's been gone for almost ten years now." Bart detected the sadness in his voice. "My son's back East. He's a teacher at a college up in Vermont. Could have been a helluva fisherman, that kid. He tried learning how to build rods—you know, take after the old man—but he just didn't have the knack for it. Too much time spent with his nose in a book."

The two of them talked through lunch, then went back to the shed to work through the afternoon. As the light began to fade, Bart glanced at his watch and said he should be thinking about heading back. They set about putting away the tools and storing the planed strips on the top shelf, gently bundled together. Before heading to the car, Bart made plans for his next visit. He told Pharis it might be two weeks before he got back, but he'd send a letter to confirm a date. Pharis reassured him that he was welcome anytime and added, "I don't go many places these days." Bart sensed loneliness.

The road to Mt. Lebanon was nearly empty. Only the occasional car or buggy passed him. Bart couldn't get his mind off the day. He replayed all he had been taught but kept focusing on the comment Pharis made just before the final goodbye. "Too bad you went into banking, Bart. You'd be a helluva rod maker. Saw it in you the first time you put a plane in your hands." Bart couldn't, or didn't want to, push the comment away.

Over the next two months, he made the trek to Kittanning every two weeks. After the planing was finished, Pharis taught him how to glue the strips together, stain and varnish the rod, and wrap the line guides. The most difficult operation for Bart was attaching the cork rings and spinning the butt section on a foot-pedal lathe to shape it. That required balancing a four-foot stick so it would spin without a wobble. Attaching the reel seat and the guides was a breeze compared with shaping the handle. Before applying the varnish, Bart printed a message along the rod just above the handle: "Laurel Creek Special." The final step was to construct a leather rod case. He had his wife Pat sew a canvas bag for the rod.

The day Bart arrived to pick up the finished rod, he brought his reel along to give the rod a test. Standing in the side yard, Bart pulled the line through the guides, gave Pharis an optimistic nod, and began. As Bart watched the rod flex forward and back, his attention was diverted by Pharis's laughter.

"I'm sorry, son. Don't take this the wrong way, but you need some work on that casting stroke," Pharis offered. Bart began to laugh as well. "Let me give you a suggestion. Grab the rod with just your thumb and the middle two fingers of your hand." Bart did as he was told and tried casting again.

He almost threw the rod out of his hand. "Try it again, only this time don't yank the rod back and forth so hard. That will help you control it."

Again, Bart lifted the line and gently eased the rod through the cast. He could feel the difference immediately. Everything slowed down. The rod worked effortlessly. Bart turned to Pharis and said, "Amazing!"

Pharis gave him a thumbs-up sign. "Sure looks like you've built a beauty for a first effort." Bart was elated.

They packed up the rod and went to the front porch. Over a glass of tea, student and teacher talked about their time together over the past few months. Before he left, Bart informed Pharis that it might be a while before he could get back to start a new rod, but he would send a letter once he knew more.

Over the next year, Bart assisted Pharis in completing several rods that had been special orders from customers at Farlow's. A few months after the last rod was finished, Bart received in the bank mail one day a large envelope inside of which was an unopened letter and Pharis's little brown book. Bart was puzzled by this, since Pharis had died more than a month earlier. The address on the inner envelope read simply "Bart Schoeppner, Mt. Lebanon." Pulling out a single page, he unfolded and read it:

> Bart,
>
> Since you are reading this letter, I obviously have moved on to somewhere else. I hope it's a nice place. Over the past months, I have greatly enjoyed working with you. And since my son has no use for

the equipment and tools, and all the others I've apprenticed now have equipment of their own, I'd like you to have them. I have informed my son of this, and he agrees. All you need do is contact him at the address below and make arrangements to pick up the stuff in the shed. I know you'll put all of it to good use.

Bart was stunned. He immediately thought, why me? His excitement was tempered by the fact that he felt undeserving of such a gift. He didn't know what to do. All of this was followed by selfish thoughts. Who would answer his questions now? What's the proper mixture of oil and stain for the varnish? How, exactly, do you measure the flexibility of a glued section? On and on the questions flowed. He picked up the book of charts and began thumbing through the pages. He wondered how many others before him had done the same thing. He knew that many apprentice rod makers had started with this book, and now he had it. As a second thought, he realized that although he had the book, he would probably never attain the knowledge or skills that rod making demanded. Those belonged to Pharis.

Three weeks later, he received a letter from Frank Pharis's son Jason. He was going to be at the Pharis house in a week to pack up his father's belongings and wondered if Bart wanted to come and clear out the shed. Bart immediately phoned the Osgoods to see if he could coax one of them into letting him use their truck and perhaps help him load the stuff.

On the appointed day, Bart and Carlton met Jason at his father's house. As they walked to the shed, Jason said, "Dad was very clear about giving you this stuff, Bart. You must have made quite an impression on him."

"Jason, I—well, I feel that all this should be yours. All you have to do is say the word and we'll just get back in the truck and head home."

Jason laughed. "Oh, no, I wouldn't have any idea what to do with this stuff. I know how to use some of it, but I'd never take the time to do something with it. No, I totally agree with Dad that this stuff should go to someone who will use it." Jason unlocked the bolt on the door and held it open for them. Following them in, he stopped in the doorway. "Look, I'm going to leave you two to this. I'll be in the house if you need me." As he started to leave, he added, "If you want to drive your truck back here to load up, that's fine."

Bart stopped him with a question. "Jason, you want the workbench left here, right?"

"Nope. If you think you can haul it out of here, go right ahead."

Carlton was roaming through the shed picking up pieces of bamboo, looking at the planing forms, pulling newly glued sections of rods off the drying racks. Watching him, Bart could imagine this was how he must have behaved the first time Pharis showed him the workshop. Carlton said, "Bart, there must be twenty sections of rods up here. What are you going to do with them?"

Bart shrugged. "I don't know. I still can't believe Pharis wanted me to have all this. This is a man's whole life, here in this building, and I'm supposed to take it home with me? It just doesn't feel right somehow."

"Look, Bart, you heard what Jason said. He doesn't have any use for it. And you can't just throw all this out as trash." Carlton walked over to where Bart stood running his hand up and down a strip of bamboo still lying in a planing form. "What say I go get the truck and you start thinking about how we should pack this." Bart nodded.

While he waited for Carlton to return, Bart strolled around the edges of the workbench gently touching the tools. He checked the edge on a plane he took off the shelf. He picked through the culm in the stock barrel. Without Pharis around, everything seemed to be just sticks and tools. His daydream was broken by the sound of the truck door being slammed. Carlton bounded into the shed. "Okay, partner, where do we start? The workbench, right?"

"Yeah, I guess we should put the big stuff in first. Let's set everything else over here next to the tools and see if we can get this bench out the door," Bart said hesitantly. Before they could move the bench, he and Carlton had to back out the bolt screws anchoring it to the floor. To their surprise, the bench slid easily between the door jambs and onto the bed of the truck. As they re-entered the shed, Bart pointed out to Carlton the grooves Pharis had worn into the wooden floor around the outline of the bench. They wrapped all the planes, planing forms, chisels, and calipers in burlap and stored them in a wooden box they found underneath the shelves. Next they slid the barrels of culm onto the truck. The most difficult items to pack were Pharis's partially assembled rods stretched across the racks. Bart decided to carry them on his lap for the ride home.

After tying down all the equipment on the truck, the two men stood in the now-empty shed. A few remaining piles of sawdust and the lights that hung around the walls gave Bart a strong feeling of emptiness. Before starting for home, they walked up to the back door and knocked. Jason appeared at the screen door. "All done?" He stepped out onto the porch. "I know you feel odd about this, Bart, but believe me, it's fine. This is what he wanted, and if there's one thing I know for sure, you don't go against his wishes."

The three men shook hands, and Jason returned inside. Carlton was about to start the truck when Jason ran out of the house and stopped them. He held a leather rod tube in his hand. He walked around the side of the truck to where Bart was sitting. "Hey, you want this too? I think this was my dad's fishing rod."

Bart was confounded by this generosity. After handing Carlton the rod pieces from his lap, he stepped out of the truck. "Jason, I can't take this. This was your father's. Even if you don't use it, it belongs in your family, not mine. You've already been too generous as it is."

Jason tried to talk him into changing his mind, explaining that there was no one who would use it, but Bart stood firm. Eventually, they shook hands, and Bart climbed back into the truck.

Bart again cradled the glued but unfinished rod pieces across his lap, the last efforts of Frank Pharis, Rod Builder. "Let's go," Bart insisted. Jason was at the back of the truck and waved good-bye.

Carlton dropped the truck into gear and headed down the gravel path leading out to the road. Shortly after turning onto the highway that would take them back west, Carlton turned to Bart. "Partner, you just hit the mother lode."

"Carlton, don't say anything more about all this. I feel as if I'm looting my father's grave."

"Look, the guy wanted you to have all this, didn't he? I can see how you feel strange about it, but it's not as if you weaseled your way into this situation. This was Pharis's decision. It's the way Jason wants it too," Carlton added, trying to ease his friend's troubled thoughts.

"I suppose so, but something just doesn't feel right." Carlton shook his head in disbelief.

When they arrived at Bart's house, they faced the problem of where to put everything. While Bart went inside to let Pat know he was home, Carlton began untying the ropes. Circling around to the back side of the truck bed, he grabbed the rope holding one of the wooden boxes to slide it toward him. He pulled but the box wouldn't move. He pulled harder. It only slightly budged. He climbed up into the bed of the truck and immediately saw the problem. Something was wedged between the two boxes. Pushing one box forward while pulling the other, he saw it and yelled for Bart.

Bart came out the side door of the house and asked what the commotion was about. Carlton waved him over and pulled him up on the bed. "Look."

Bart looked between the boxes. "Damn!" He reached down and grabbed the leather strap. Frank's rod.

"He must have stuck it back here when you were getting back in the truck and we were fiddling with all the rod pieces," Carlton concluded.

"Damn," Bart said again but more emphatically.

"What are you going to do?"

"I don't know." Bart sounded overwhelmed. "I just do not know."

Bart took the rod and laid it across the seat in the cab with the pieces he had been holding. He joined Carlton in unloading the truck and carrying everything to the garage. As they reached into the cab for the last few items, Bart again was faced with what to do with Pharis's rod. "I've got to send it back, Carlton. It just doesn't feel right."

Carlton walked around the truck to his friend's side. "Bart, for once in your life, can't you just accept what's happened?"

"I know, you're going to tell me this was Jason's decision and I need to accept it. I might feel better if Pharis had mentioned the rod in his letter, but he didn't. That makes me think he wanted it to be for his son, not some smart-ass banker from Pittsburgh. I've got to send it back," Bart repeated.

"Bart, even if that is what Pharis intended, his son made the decision to put this in the trunk. Did you think of that?" Carlton grabbed Bart by the shoulders and forced him face-to-face. "Why did Pharis build fly rods? I'll tell you—so people could fish with them. Yeah, yeah, I know all about the craftsmanship side of this. You've talked about it as if it's all there is in the world. But you've also got to realize that to build a rod and never use it is like tying flies and cutting off the hook." Bart remained unconvinced. Finally, Carlton added, "Look, don't send it back right away. Give it a few days at least."

Bart agreed to wait a day or two. The next morning, he went to the garage and began sorting some of the equipment. Although he tried to ignore the leather case, he finally opened it. He pulled the rod bag out of the tube and let it slide down the rod pieces. The reel seat on the lower section was tiger maple. He had never seen a finer piece of wood. The rod it-self was beautifully maintained but showed definite signs of wear. There were two tips in the bag, though one was shorter than the other. The bamboo was stained a rich auburn color, and the guides were wrapped in swirled red and yellow thread. Bart joined the ferrules of one of the tips and gave the rod a quick flex. He was surprised at the length of the rod. Standing it vertically by his side, he estimated it was little more than seven feet tall. Maybe seven and a half. The cork handle was darkly stained from dirt on a sweaty hand being pressed into it.

It was a nice rod, though he had expected something even finer. He assumed that anyone who had devoted his entire life to building rods for other people would have the best for himself. He looked at the printing on the shaft: 1903—7' 1/2". From the lightness of the rod, Bart figured it to be a C weight. He wondered if the 1903 was a model number or the year it was made. There was no way to tell, but the rod certainly looked that old. Bart slid it back into the sleeve and rod case and carried it into the house. There was a note on the kitchen table. "Jack called and said every-one was meeting at the cabin on Saturday." The solution dawned on him.

He left early that Saturday morning for the cabin, his new rod and Pharis's old rod resting across the backseat. He still felt uncomfortable about having Pharis's rod, but he knew how to make it all seem right, or at least how to ease his own feelings. The pull-off along the road was nearly full. Carlton's truck and Jack's and Doc's cars were already there. He guessed they probably had come out last night.

He grabbed the rods off the seat and headed down the path. He could hear their voices and smell the aroma of bacon long before the cabin came into sight. As he walked up the slight grade to where the group was sitting around the campfire, Carlton was the first to speak. "Hey, Bart, you're just in time for breakfast. Let me throw some more bacon in the pan."

Bart leaned the rod cases against the side of the cabin and walked over and sat down. "Just a little, Carlton. I ate something earlier. I will take a cup of that coffee, though." Bart walked into the cabin to get his cup, all the while thinking about how and when to give Charlie the rod. By the time he returned, bacon was being forked onto plates. He circled the group, poured himself a cup of coffee, and took a seat.

"Hey, there's bacon here for you," Jack said. Bart acknowledged it with a nod. "Bart, last night Carlton told us all about the stuff you got from your rod maker friend. Seems you hit the jackpot. Did you bring your new rod?"

"Yeah, I thought I'd give it a try today," Bart responded between sips.

"Is that it over there?" Jack continued.

"Yeah."

"Why are there two cases, then? Did you build two rods?" Jack asked.

Nonchalantly, Bart said, "No, the other one is Charlie's."

The group fell silent, except for Charlie. "What?" he yelled, lunging off his log. "Did you say the other one is for me?"

Bart smiled at him as Charlie bobbed up and down. "Yeah, the other rod's for you. Go have a look."

Charlie didn't know if he should or not. He looked at his father. "Dad?"

"Don't look at me, son. I have no idea what he's talking about," Jack said, with a look of surprise on his face that was outshone only by Charlie's.

"Charlie, it's okay. Go ahead," Bart said. Bart looked at Carlton and confirmed what he was thinking with a wink.

Charlie looked again at his dad, who merely tipped his head toward the rod. Charlie took off so fast that he caught his toe on one of the rocks supporting the fire grate and dumped the pan of bacon on the ground. Scrambling to his feet, he rushed to the cabin and stopped in front of the two rod cases. Without turning around, he yelled, "Which one is it?"

Bart answered him. "The one on the right."

Charlie grabbed the strap and turned slowly around, clutching the case against his chest. He looked at the four men sliding the rock back into place. He was nearly breathless.

"Come on, Charlie, let's see what you got," Jack urged.

Charlie resumed his seat next to his father, still pressing the leather case against his chest. Then he lay the case across his lap and stroked it gently.

"Well, are you going to open it or just hold it in your lap all day?" Jack asked.

Charlie slid the cap off the end of the case and began inching out the bag. Jack helped him join one of the tips with the butt section. While Charlie eyed the rod up and down, Jack slipped the other tip back into the bag and then into the case. Jack looked at Bart. "I don't know what to say." He turned back to watch Charlie, then again to Bart. "Thanks."

Bart whispered, "You're welcome."

"Oh, Bart, thank you so much. Dad, can I use this today? Can I go with you today and use this?" he asked.

"Son, don't you think we better get a reel and some line for the rod first?" Jack could see Charlie's shoulders slump. Charlie hadn't thought about that. "I'll tell you what. You help clean up the stuff from breakfast, and we'll drive back into town to Smitty's and see if we can get a reel and line."

Charlie handed Jack the rod. Taking a position next to the fire, he looked at the group and asked, "Does anyone want anything else before I start cleaning up?" Everyone laughed. Charlie didn't get it.

Carlton spoke up. "Charlie, why don't you let us get all this. You get that rod back in the case and get going with your dad. This is too good of a day to waste cleaning grease from a frying pan."

Charlie looked at his father. Jack answered the plea in Charlie's eyes. "What can I say? Let's go."

Doc moved over next to Jack. "Say, Jack—or maybe I should ask Charlie—do you mind if I have a look at that? If you trust me to put it away for you, you and your dad can get started right away." Jack passed the rod to Doc.

Charlie was partway up the path before he realized Jack wasn't with him. He turned and yelled, "Come on, Dad."

Jack yelled back, "I've got to get the car keys. I'll be there in a minute." They heard a faint "hurry up" echo off the trees. Jack turned and said, "Bart," but he couldn't find the words to finish the sentence.

Bart looked up at him. "You better get going, or he'll try to leave without you."

Jack chuckled and headed for the cabin. The rest of them watched Jack as he headed along the path, and they acknowledged his good-bye with a wave of hands. Suddenly he stopped and called to them. "Hey, what weight is that rod?" Doc looked down at the handle but saw it wasn't marked. Bart called to Jack that it was a C. A wave of the hand let them know he had heard the answer.

Although Bart was aware of the conversation among Doc, Julian, and Carlton as they passed the rod back and forth, his mind wandered to Frank Pharis. Bart had never been someone to believe in fate, but this all seemed too perfect. He wondered if somewhere, somehow, Pharis was aware of what Bart had done with his rod.

After the three men completed their perusal of the rod, Julian spoke. "Hey, fellas, rather than putting this back in the case, what about putting it in the cabin rack next to Jack's rod?" Everyone agreed. Julian had another idea. "Does anyone have anything we could use as a fly wallet for Charlie? I thought maybe we could each stick a couple of flies in it and have it waiting for him when he gets back."

Doc spoke up. "I keep a set of first-aid gear in the car that's inside of a leather bag. Think that would work?" No one responded. "Let me go get it. Let's give it a try."

While Doc went to his car, the other three took the rod inside. Julian leaned it against the wall in the corner while Carlton took his knife and began cutting a slot into the upper section of the rod rack for the new addition. Bart began shaping a piece of leather to fit across the opening to hold the rod into the rack. Doc returned to the cabin and called everyone over to the table in the center of the room. The leather bag was about the size of a kid's marble bag and was closed with a drawstring. It wasn't a wallet, but it would certainly do for the moment. While Doc, Bart, and Julian sorted through the flies and dropped some into the bag, Carlton finished the notch and hammered the strap into the rack. Grabbing the rod, he slipped it into the base and secured it with the strap. He stepped back to admire the new addition. Julian hung the fly bag over the nail in front of the rod.

Their work completed, they slipped their own rods out of the rack and headed out to the fire to clean up. As Doc and Bart reset the fire stones and Julian and Carlton washed the pan and plates in the water barrel, they talked about how Bart had come to have the rod. Bart's feelings about returning the rod to Jason were now gone. He knew the rod was where it was supposed to be. He also knew that Frank Pharis would be pleased by his decision.

After the chores were done, Bart removed his new rod from its case and began attaching his reel to it. Julian and Carlton came over to admire his work. Doc joined them a few minutes later. As the four of them headed down to the creek, Charlie was the topic of discussion. They laughed about his reaction and his stumbling over the rock. They wondered if he and Jack had arrived at Smitty's yet. At the water's edge, they decided that Doc and Bart would head downstream and Julian and his brother upstream. Before they split up, Julian lifted his flask to the others. "The usual, gentlemen?" They nodded in agreement with flasks pulled from pockets.

A couple of hours later, Bart headed for shore with the excuse that he had to pee. Instead, he began quietly walking down the path back toward the cabin to see if Jack and Charlie had returned. He figured Jack would take Charlie to the area straight down from the cabin for his first real experience with fly fishing. As he approached the spot, he heard voices from midstream. "Charlie, you need to slow down. You're not switching flies off a mule." There was a pause. "There you go. Now you're getting the hang of it." Bart edged closer, trying to stay behind the trees. About then he noticed he wasn't alone. Not more than fifty yards away, the Osgoods were playing the same spy game. They acknowledged each other with a wave. Bart moved his arm back and forth as if he had a rod in his hand and exaggeratedly nodded his head in an attempt to communicate his approval of Charlie's casting. Julian's return nod let him know the message had been received. They watched for a while and then headed back to their spots in the creek.

Not having a son of his own, Bart had vicarious feelings of parenthood seeing the pleasure Charlie gained from the rod. Everyone watched Charlie develop into a fisherman who occasionally outfished all of them. Watching the tip of Pharis's old rod gracefully bend above the bushes made Bart realize that the rod was where it should be—in the hands of a boy, fishing in a stream.

> *I had a chance to watch a blue heron fish the shallows this evening. I had gone down to the creek to get a bucket of water and noticed it standing dead still along the far bank by the rock field. It makes you wonder what fish see looking up through the water. Do they see the shape of a bird? An odd stick? Maybe there are little things on those long, spindly legs that draw fish closer. I can't imagine fish voluntarily swimming toward the bird. Something must lure them.*
>
> *I've seen these kinds of birds before but never one up close. They are astoundingly effective, waiting without*

movement and suddenly thrusting their long neck into the water to grab a fish. I must have watched this particular bird for close to a half hour, and out of maybe twenty tries, it caught a fish at least half the time. I wish I was that efficient, getting a fish every other cast. But I don't need to fish for basic survival. It's amazing to watch how the bird flips the fish around with its beak until it's aimed headfirst down the throat. I've even heard it said that the parents regurgitate whole fish for the chicks. Now that's something I'd like to see.

Bart, June 1952

Epilogue

I looked back through the list of names in the journal. What an American collection of lineages. I continued on through the pages. The entries were sporadic, often no more than a handful per year. Most of them were about days spent fishing on the Laurel. I was particularly taken by a piece that explained the pains these men had to take to keep their equipment in proper working order. One entry was about the decision to install a set of pegs on the wall opposite the fireplace where they could loosely hang their greased silk lines overnight to "cure." There was a discussion of gut leaders and hook size. I kept thinking that the terms and materials would be different, but if one were to step into a conversation going on anywhere in the world among a group of fly fishermen, they'd be talking about the same subjects. Another interesting piece included the favorite flies among the group.

June 5, 1935
Over a recent dinner, the subject of favorite flies was broached. It is here recorded the three choices for each member of The Society:

Julian	E. Fredrick
Silver Doctor	La Belle
Cow Dung	White Miller
Queen of the Water	Reuben Wood

Carlton	Barton
Great Dun	Gray Hackle
Stone King	Red Fox
Polka	Coachman

Jackson
Red Fox
Black Gnat
Quill Gordon

Queen of the Water? Reuben Wood? These were flies I had never heard of. I could pretty much guess what a Gray or Brown Hackle would look like, maybe even a Great Dun, but I couldn't, in my wildest imagination, come up with any possibility for a Cow Dung. A what? Kelly and I later were able to find a picture of a Cow Dung in Mary Orvis Marbury's book on flies and their histories. It was a chocolate brown fly with a trim body, two extended brown wings above dark hackle, and a set of antennae extended out along the eyes. It was a damn good-looking fly, one I might have to give a go some day.

The overall tone of the entries gave me a feeling of being among true gentlemen. It was the way they expressed their thoughts, the words they selected for describing the changing seasons, the colors of the trout, the *"smoke from a sizzling frying pan, wafting through the oaks with hints of mint and butter."* Then quite suddenly, another picture emerged.

July 4, 1938

The game is afoot! After much struggle to bring the entire group together, basically through threats, we assemble this day amid a grand plan to engage the trout in a new fashion. The Osgoods instigated the game, and it took little persuasion for all to agree. In this we established our Independence Day Celebration. The rules are thus:

1. Two teams of fishermen will be established by drawing lots. The last name drawn will serve on both teams.

2. Each team will then, among themselves, designate an order of fishermen. The first designee of one team will then be paired with his counterpart from the other team.

3. Each team will create a "Sacred Cache" of flies whose total number must be one dozen. The choice of flies is totally at the discretion of the team.

4. Promptly at 8:50 A.M., all will assemble around the fire pit. At that time a bottle of MacCallan's shall be opened, drinks poured for each member, and these consumed at 9:00 A.M. The first pair of fishermen will immediately depart for the water after selecting a fly from the team's Sacred Cache.

5. Each pair must fish within sight of each other. When the first fish is brought to the net, the pair will return to the cabin, at which time the person catching the fish will consume another dram of scotch.

6. *Once the shot is consumed, the second pair will depart for the water. This pattern will continue until the allotted time has elapsed.*

7. *If one of the pair should lose his fly, he must wait for the other until a fish is caught or the second fly is lost. However, if the fly can be retrieved, that fisherman may resume the challenge. Any unretrievable fly cannot be replaced, and that fisherman, or those fishermen, shall deduct one fish from the team's tally at the end of the day.*

8. *Upon the close of the four o'clock hour, a tally shall be made in the following manner: the total number of fish landed by each team, minus any lost flies, shall be multiplied by the number of flies remaining in the team's Sacred Cache.*

9. *The losing team shall acknowledge its position in the order of merit among The Society by maintaining, for one full season, an adequate supply of Scotch in the cabin for the members.*

10. *It should be noted that those members not part of the pair in the river are not in any manner restricted from continuing to toast our beloved country. God Bless America!*

My first thought after reading this entry was that The Society's members certainly knew how to enjoy themselves. I wondered if the Treetop Tavern was around in their day. They'd fit right in. An additional notation entered at the bottom of the page read *First Order of Merit: Osgood, Osgood, Schoeppner. Second Order of Merit: Wheatley, Langsenkamp, Schoeppner.*

Another entry was about Carlton Osgood and his brother, Julian, climbing on top of the roof to howl at the moon.

We had to chase the Osgood brothers off the roof. We should have known to be ready for this, but since the vernal equinox doesn't always come on a Saturday or Sunday when someone is usually here, we forget about it.

Apparently, Julian and Carlton started this when they were boys after being told a story about a wolf born on the first day of spring and how this wolf grew up as the best hunter in the north woods. The Osgoods told us about all this the evening we first found them up there. When they came down from the roof, they told us they had been doing this howling deal every year since to celebrate having survived another winter. This would have been understandable of kids, or maybe even men if they at sometime in their lives had been a pair of backwoodsmen surviving by their wits and skills. But this is a pair of real estate lawyers whose idea of roughing it is spending more than three days at the cabin without going into town to The Stockade for a steak.

This time when we chased them down so we could go back to sleep, they said they had both fallen on particularly hard times with their fishing and were trying to commune with the forest gods to shine more favorably upon them. Of course, the two rows of Highlander bottles we found lined up on the table next morning had nothing to do with it.

While Jack and I struggled to shake off the grogginess of interrupted sleep and began our stroll down to the river, we were greeted by Carlton and Julian coming back, each with a creel full of fish. As we stopped to admire their catch, Julian almost condescendingly said, "See, it worked."

This doesn't bode well for the rest of us.

Barton
August 10, 1940

A 1941 entry noted the tragedy at Pearl Harbor. I was a little surprised, though maybe I shouldn't have been, that the next entry was dated 1945. Obviously the war had impacted the time the men could spend at the cabin. However, as I began reading, it was not at all what I had expected.

> *It is with great sadness that we enter into this record the loss of Jackson's son, Charlie, to the war. The telegram from the War Department arrived a week ago. Charlie was nineteen and died in the Ardennes Forest of Belgium.*
>
> *Charlie and Jack started coming to the cabin to fish together when he was nine years old. It was here Jack taught Charlie the joys, skills, and routines of fly fishing. The lessons did not come easily for Charlie, but he always pursued them with great endurance and enthusiasm—the makings of a good soldier. We will always remember the day a few years later when Charlie caught Big Sam, the king of the river that none of us had been able to catch. It was early one quiet morning when we heard Charlie down by the creek yelling, "I caught Big Sam! I caught Big Sam!" We raced the hundred yards down to the pool where Big Sam always hid, and there was Charlie in the stream holding Big Sam down on the gravel. I don't think there was a dry eye among us when Charlie asked Jack if it would be okay to let Big Sam go. And that's what Charlie did. With one powerful swish of his tail, Big Sam headed home.*
>
> *Now, as we all suffer Jack's loss, we must wonder why God has taken from us the boy who committed an act of kindness from which we all learned so much. At that moment, we all more clearly understood the phrase "From the mouths of babes comes the wisdom of the ages." As a dedication to Charlie and Jackson, we have placed two photographs on the wall next to where Charlie's*

rod remains in the rack. One is of him and his dad standing
in the Laurel the day he caught Big Sam; the other is of
the two of them with their arms around each other's
shoulders, Charlie in uniform, inside the Pittsburgh train
station.
    We have renamed that spot on the river Charlie's Pool.

Bart
January 20, 1945

Just as the entries about the Sacred Cache and the howling Osgood brothers had made me laugh, this one made my arms and neck tingle. It made the sacrifices of those who fought the war become real for me. I vowed at that moment to visit Charlie's Pool before I returned home.

Throughout the journal other members' deaths were noted, often with a simple written tribute. The first to pass on was Barton Schoeppner in 1954, a victim of cancer. Carlton Osgood died in 1958 of a heart attack, and his brother Julian in 1961. The death of Jackson Langsenkamp was the most tragic.

Jack started coming again a few years after burying
Charlie, but it never was the same for him. He spent too
much time alone for his own good, sitting on top of the
rock above Charlie's Pool. Eventually he stopped coming
all together. I couldn't get him to come despite calls to that
nature. His presence was always here, as his rod still hung
on the rack. I finally knew he wouldn't be back when I dis-
covered he had been here and taken the pictures of him
and Charlie. The deepest sadness I've ever known was the
day Frances called to say that Jack had taken his own life.
    Jack was buried holding the picture of the two of
them taken the day Charlie caught Big Sam. I hope there's

*a cabin and trout stream in heaven so they can hang up
their picture and again fish together.*

*Each time I see the news of more young men dying
in Vietnam, I wonder, at what price? How many other
fathers and mothers have lost the will to continue on and
considered Jack's path to resolution?*

August 1971

I read on but struggled to shake off the death of Jackson Langsenkamp. How tragic. The entries for the 1970s and later were sporadic, with entire years passing without anything written in the journal.

I shut the book and laid it on my chest with my arms folded across it. Closing my eyes, I began picturing the men sitting around the fire pit eating trout and toasting fish won and lost; laughter echoing through the trees as someone told an FDR joke; the last man awake adding extra logs to the fireplace before climbing the stairs to the cots; thick canvas and wool wading pants drying on nails hammered into the outside walls of the cabin; an interior wall rack holding bamboo rods stored until the next day; the framed pictures of Jackson Langsenkamp and his son Charlie hanging by the rack; the Osgoods howling on the roof. On and on these visions came as I fell asleep among images of men I'd never meet and times I'd never know.

At breakfast the next day, I told Kelly and Lisa about some of the journal entries I had read. Kelly spit a chunk of pancake onto the table when I told him one of the flies was called a Cow Dung. He smiled broadly at Lisa's tilted glance when I described the howling Osgoods.

Later that morning, Kelly and I climbed into his Jeep and

headed back to the Laurel. We took another look through the cabin but found nothing else that would have belonged to The Society's members. As we walked out of the cabin, grabbing our rods where we had leaned them against a tree, I stopped Kelly. "There's another spot I want to see. Remember that story I told you about Charlie Langsenkamp? I wonder if we can find the pool where he caught Big Sam."

"Where did they say it was?"

"I think I read that it was about a hundred yards downstream. But downstream from where?" I wondered aloud. "Kelly, the journal said they heard Charlie yell when he hooked Big Sam. In that case, it can't be very far. Come on."

We took off toward the river and began walking downstream. When we'd gone what we thought was a hundred yards or so, we began looking for the wall of rock. Which bank was it on? Since we were both in our waders, we decided the best way to look for it was from the water. In we went. I headed downstream, and Kelly headed back the way we had come. Shortly, I heard Kelly yell, "Down here!"

I waded upstream as fast as my legs would allow me to push against the current. When I reached Kelly's side, he pointed to my left at a wall of rock almost totally hidden by an overhang of bushes. It fit the description. We walked downstream to where we could get up the bank and then back to the edge. We were able to pull the bushes back and fairly effortlessly stretch out on the rock above the pool just as members of The Society had done. Peering down into the water, we could see several small fish cruise in and out from the undercut to grab nymphs and larvae as they floated by. We were amazed at the speed with which the fish darted out and back. Each lunge took only seconds. Kelly was impressed.

"Cool!" As I took my eyes off the drama below, I noticed something under Kelly's hand.

"What's that?" I said, pushing his hand aside.

"Where?"

"There, by your hand. It looks like something in the rock." I rubbed it with my hand. Slowly, the dirt flaked away and the letter "r" appeared. Both of us began rubbing away the crusted dirt, and one by one more letters came forth. We pushed ourselves up to get a better view to read the words—Charlie's Pool. I was stunned. I had expected to find the pool but not this. I now knew more of how Jack Langsenkamp spent his final days at the Laurel.

We wouldn't fish here.

That day we did fish other spots along the Laurel, catching what were likely thirtieth- or fortieth-generation descendants of Big Sam and his harem. Over lunch, eaten on the rock above Charlie's Pool, Kelly and I speculated about the men who had built the cabin in the woods, and how their interests and hopes were not unlike our own. As we talked, I had visions of the men emerging through the trees in their waxed canvas fishing pants, bamboo rods in hand, their faces beaming in anticipation. I felt if I concentrated hard enough I could make the apparitions materialize. I wanted to talk with them, share a drink, ask them about the Sacred Cache contest . . . just fish with them. Kelly and I spent the rest of the day fishing while I told him my stories about the men between fish. I cannot recall a more enjoyable day fishing.

The final day of my visit, we went to Spring Creek, but it wasn't the same. On the drive back, I asked Kelly for one more chance to see the Laurel. I didn't go to the cabin, though I'm not sure why. My guess is I had concluded the cabin wasn't what made the journal entries so real for me. It had served our needs by protecting and eventually surrendering the book that became the apex of the time Kelly and I spent together. It dominated our conversation prior to my departure for home the next day. The miles of interstate rolled past unnoticed as my mind tumbled back to the sights and smells of the Laurel.

Months later, in the middle of winter, I received a package from Kelly. Inside was a letter, a photocopy of a newspaper piece, and a photograph.

Dear Cole,

I thought you'd like to know about some of the things that have happened since you were here. I was in town the other day and stopped by to see a friend at the Ligonier *Echo*. I thought maybe he could help us find out something about the men whose names were in the journal. He tapped into the morgue files at the paper, but the only thing he could come up with was the copy of Doctor Wheatley's obituary I've sent along in this package. Once you read it, you'll understand why I did what I did with the journal.

After reading Wheatley's obit, I contacted the president of the local Trout Unlimited chapter about the journal. He was thrilled, especially since Wheatley was a cofounder of the chapter. You'll be pleased to know he was able to get the book placed in the Ligonier Historical Society's archives. The members asked me to tell them the story of how we found it, and I even read a couple of the entries at a meeting one night. They were absolutely amazed. A few days later, we sent it off to the state's preservationist at Harrisburg for restoration. Eventually it will be returned for the archives to keep. I knew you'd want to know that it was safe. If I can, I'll try to get photocopies of the pages and send them to you once the book is returned.

The photograph is an early Christmas present from Lisa and me. Also, when are you coming back to see us?

Tight lines,
Kelly

The photograph was of me with my legs dangling over the edge of the rock above Charlie's Pool. At the bottom of the frame was a small shadow box in which Kelly had mounted the Quill Gordon he found in the cabin. He had even sanded off the rust.

I set the picture on the table and picked up Wheatley's obituary. The date at the corner of the page was May 5, 1989. Above the text was a picture of a man with a white downturned mustache that curled around the corner of each side of the mouth. The mustache added to a long, angular thin face perched above a polka-dot bow tie. I thought he looked more like a cowboy than a doctor. Take away the bow tie and replace it with a flannel shirt and leather vest and he'd be a perfect Zane Grey hero. His smiling eyes, though, showed a kindness that I'm sure made many kids and their parents much more at ease about seeing the doctor.

Dr. E. Fredrick Wheatley, 87, died Thursday, at his home. Services will be held at St. Catherine's Cathedral, Saturday, at 1:00 P.M. Visitation will be at Berry & Kerr Mortuary in Ligonier from 6:00 to 8:00 P.M. Friday.

A graduate of the Medical College of the University of Pittsburgh, Dr. Wheatley moved his practice from Pittsburgh to his office on the Diamond in Ligonier in 1930. While serving the medical needs of the residents of Ligonier and surrounding areas, Dr. Wheatley served on the Board of Regents of St. Catherine's Cathedral and School, was a former president of the Kiwanis, sponsored the annual Christmas toy collection for the Westmoreland County Guardians Home, and was cofounder of the Loyalhanna Chapter of Trout Unlimited.

In addition to his philanthropic ventures, Dr. Wheatley published several poems and short stories in magazines such as *Sports Afield* and *Woodland Hunter* under the pen name Gordon Quill. He was known to hunt and fish many of the Laurel Mountains and once each summer hosted a fishing day for children at the cabin owned by The Gentlemen's Society of Angling. He was the last living member of The Society. He was the widower of Carol Grace Horton. Wheatley is survived by his daughter, Barbara Underwood, and three grandchildren.

That's it? I thought. That's all there was to say about a man who had obviously given so much to others and the sport he loved? It seemed terribly incomplete, almost casual. Of course, the cub reporter who had written the obit hadn't had a chance to interact with the man I had come to know from reading the journal. I immediately pegged Wheatley as the author of all the literary-quality entries in the journal whose authors were not identified. Anyone who could publish poetry and stories couldn't avoid a degree of flare in his words. Certainly, The Sportsman's Creed was penned by his hand.

I again began thinking about these five men and their lives. There was a richness here known only to a few, those people who find their serenity and value beyond the walls and gadgets of human creation. These men were equally as exceptional as any hero I had ever learned about. Gentle men chasing a simple dream, to find in their woods a quiet meaning to their lives. And they had fun doing it. There was tragedy here too. That makes their lives all the more powerful. Without the tragedy, triumph is harder to recognize. I now realize more fully that which of these we focus on is a matter of choice, not fate.

It's funny how a fishing trip, a chance to engage new waters, turns out to be far more than a few trout and time with old friends. After reading the journal of The Gentlemen's Society, I felt as if I had been on my best fishing trip ever, one that had lasted for decades. Certainly my circle of friends and acquaintances had grown far beyond Kelly and Lisa. I could feel every fish the members caught wriggling in my hand, their need to oil the fibers of a silk line and hang it on a wall peg overnight for the next day's fishing, the tying of flies by kerosene lamp at a table sitting in the corner next to the fireplace. I recognized these men, having met them at different times in my own travels. The unique aspect of this trip was that I met them all in one evening.

The last entry gave me some clue to how The Society ended.

> *It's hard to believe that when we first started venturing to the woods, only the main highway in town was improved, and it was merely rolled tar and gravel. Now I can hear cars from the cabin as they flow through our valley. The solitude I step into here is diminished by their drone. Such is the price of progress. Such is the price of regress.*
>
> *I now invest more time reflecting on the almost forty years I've walked in the Laurel. The quest for brook trout still pervades my soul, though tangentially one fish is now often sufficient to warm the deepest recesses of my memory. When in our travels in this life do we shift from battling to embracing all that surrounds us? For me it is the privity to a larger order I've gained from standing in the Laurel, rod in hand, imitating the life of a bug. It is often presented that the trout is the object of desire. I now wonder if the insect isn't the real point of engagement, for it is the means to the end. As most people eventually learn, the pursuit is far more enriching than the conquest.*
>
> *I'm having to accept that imminently I will stop coming, not so much because the desire has fled but rather due to the physical demands.*
>
> *We had a good run!*
>
> *July 20, 1972*

The final entry clarified for me what I had been unable to express except in my inner feelings—I too hear the highway now when I fish. Sadly, for me and others in this day and age, it is increasingly harder to find places where the cacophony of civilization isn't crashing and cashing in on nature. For these men, this type of intrusion must have been harder to accept, for they had known a place of pristine refuge. They were ahead of their time in seeing a river, a woods, and a remote valley in the Laurel Mountains of Pennsylvania as more than a place to make a living. It was a place where one could do as Thoreau did and choose to live purposefully, to understand what it means to draw nourishment from the marrow of life. Regularly, and especially as I fish a section of my home waters where a rock wall exists, I roll the journal entries through my mind. I feel deeply grateful for what I gained from The Gentlemen's Society of Angling. I truly believe its members are together again, sitting around a fire pit talking of fish and flies while the Osgood brothers howl from the roof. At least by now I'm sure they have discovered whether their conjecture was true that, clearly, God fly fishes.